# Differentiated Teaching and Learning in Youth Work Training

# Differentiated Teaching and Learning in Youth Work Training

Brian Belton
Simon Frost

*YMCA George Williams College, London, UK*

SENSE PUBLISHERS
ROTTERDAM/BOSTON/TAIPEI

A C.I.P. record for this book is available from the Library of Congress.

ISBN: 978-94-6091-196-5 (paperback)
ISBN: 978-94-6091-197-2 (hardback)
ISBN: 978-94-6091-198-9 (e-book)

Published by: Sense Publishers,
P.O. Box 21858,
3001 AW Rotterdam,
The Netherlands
http://www.sensepublishers.com

*Printed on acid-free paper*

# DEDICATION

This book is dedicated to the full-time students of the YMCA George Williams College (2006–2009) some of whom are pictured on the cover of this book. Many of the ideas and conclusions included in the following pages were developed working *with* and alongside them. They are gifted, generous and able youth workers. Their communities and our society are fortunate to have such an amicable and noble group accompanying young people on the start of their journey into the rest of their lives. They represent the richness youth work can bring to the world. Threats of the loss of their contribution via the demise of their profession are shadows that civil societies would seek to diminish.

# TABLE OF CONTENTS

# INTRODUCTION

While this book is primarily concerned with method and direction of teaching and tutoring youth work theory, it is also directed at a wider field practice and practitioner development within the context of higher, professional education. Although the field of professional training has grown dramatically over the last quarter of a century, surprisingly there has been little written about teaching method, content and approach with specific regard to youth workers. It has almost been taken for granted that the means and approach to initial training in related professions, for instance social work and teaching, have been and are sufficient and appropriate to youth work training/ education. This is understandable as youth work, which has been referred to as a 'para-profession' in some quarters, is a much younger discipline than other caring/welfare/educational professions, lacking influence because of its social profile, being for the most part made up of part-time and voluntary workers; full-time youth workers are a small cadre nationally compared to say the numbers involved in teaching and social work.

For all this, the practice of youth work, involving as it does a focus on essentially individuals and social groups, is bounded by the motivations of those they work with (albeit sometimes within limited options). Youth workers often come together with their clients in an apparently ad hoc, even chaotic manner. However, while maintaining a high degree of attention to the well-being and growth of those they work with, youth workers have employed a range of techniques and principals applicable across the 'people professions'. But youth work has also encompassed a number of approaches and ethical considerations that have been adopted to a level and shaped in ways that are quite exceptional to the field.

At the same time, youth work recruits from a constituency that is unique relative to related professions. Youth workers often come into higher prof-essional education without formal qualifications of any sort, not unusually carrying negative experiences of schooling and education in general. But as a group they do have a wide range of relevant experience and impressive pre-graduate, in-service training portfolios.

With this in mind it is clear that those involved in the professional training of youth workers need to develop original and appropriate attitudes in terms of their teaching methods and direction. This needs to reach beyond what has become the conventional fare of group work theory, based as it so often is, on a loose mixture of assumptions, premised on sets of vague psychoanalytic/psychotherapeutic notions (built for the most part within the social and political confines of west coast America during the Cold War era) together with a diet of relatively shallow management theory, basic psychology and some rudimentary sociology.

This being the case, while what follows does not claim to be an exhaustive methodological text, it has relevance over a range of training levels within youth work but is also pertinent to other teaching and learning situations involving professional engagement with individuals, groups and communities.

In the first part of the book Brian Belton will look at approaches and methods of teaching, focusing on the development of differentiated practice in the context of youth work training. It has been written with the wide educational constituency of recruitment to the field in mind but at the same time offers a guide and insight into differentiated teaching and learning relevant across the horizon of professional education in related spheres (such as social work).

This is followed by Simon Frost's work on the character and direction of practice. This provides a useful guide to the ethos and ethical direction of youth work via the debate relating a persistent quandary in practice; do we work 'with' or 'on' clients? This seemingly straightforward exploration skilfully and helpfully opens up the nature of youth work practice to examination and in the process offers an in depth discussion about the trajectory and purpose the professional intervention activities in and around the discipline.

Graduating from the 1960s/1970s London Dockland gang culture and football violence, Dr Brian Belton has practiced and taught youth work in, amongst other places, Bethnal Green, Glasgow, Hong Kong, Israel, America, Thailand and the Falkland Islands for the better part of four decades. A senior lecturer at the YMCA George Williams College, Brian (a sociologist, critical anthropologist and social historian) is the author of over 40 books. He is an internationally recognized authority on Gypsy and Traveller identity and has specialized in ethnic studies and Black History in his development of radical youth work theory.

CHAPTER 1

# DIFFERENTIATED TEACHING AND LEARNING IN YOUTH WORK TRAINING

> *The man who has everything figured out is probably a fool. College examinations notwithstanding, it takes a very smart fella to say 'I don't know the answer'-* Drummond, Lawrence, J., Lee, R.E. (1951) *Inherit the Wind* Ballantine, Act 1; Scene II (p. 55)

INTRODUCTION

The objective of what follows is to stimulate conversation about what in the contemporary educational environment is considered indicative of 'best practice'. In part it was motivated by comments from a number of professional youth workers, for instance,

*Youth Service training in my County is incredibly prosaic, and lacks any poetry for me - it is also not delivered by anyone passionate or inspiring, and it feels like an exercise in bureaucracy.*

*The teachers who have really inspired me (and I really enjoyed my formal education) were ones who told me stories and made me feel something.*

*Overly orchestrated learning is inherently undemocratic, and much of this is due to a lack of confidence on the part of teachers who have become institutionalised.*

Given this type of response this chapter seeks to amplify and to some extent reinterpret for the sphere of youth work training, what is recognized as differentiated teaching and learning. I hope to explore something of the rationale and justification for the same within this particular sector of higher professional education, an arena that is said to attract what has been termed 'non-traditional' learners[1]. What this in practice means is that youth work draws to its ranks a diverse and as such rich and vibrant mix of people from a wide range of backgrounds. This group, perhaps unlike those taking conventional routes into higher education, bring with them what can be experienced by those tasked to teach them, challenging often unexpected questions and perspectives. Such contributions are of course potentially breaths of fresh air, as they not unusually critique taken for granted ideas, express doubts, reservations and practically justified disbelief. In many ways this is the fuel and lubricant of new understanding and innovation, that turns the cogs of paradigm shifts. This instinctual skepticism, often arising out of raw experience, is the validation of the university as a social force for change and betterment. However, for those of us who have become reliant on the comfort of conformity to the prescribed theory that is the foundation of our own outlook and the security of regulation of accepted knowledge set in the institutional context, such nonconformity might at best be dismissed as eccentricity and at worse academic heresy.

> *A teacher is one who makes themselves progressively unnecessary.*
> – Thomas Carruthers

According to an experienced HMI/Ofsted inspector I spoke to about this subject while writing this chapter;

*The implementation of differentiated strategies in education generally is considered good practice nationally and across the field, including by the Inspectorate and teacher training institutions. Teaching that is deliberately non-differentiated or formulaic, lacking distinction is often ineffective in terms of what it is trying to achieve with diverse groups of learners; it does not actively promote the chances of appropriate differentiated learning experiences.*

This said, learner experience of training often seems to be marked out by prescribed and rigid styles and content. A youth worker in Essex told me;

*The way that teachers are taught to 'teach' by institutions usually concentrates on Key Performance Indicators (yuk) and effective ways of getting students to pass exams. Those who try their best to teach from the heart have their creativity crushed. All too often in youth work too much of the focus is placed on how many fucking accredited outcomes we can 'get' for the young people. This way of looking at things has become so endemic in training now. I almost feel a young person could get an OCN* [Open College Network accreditation] *for a disclosure of abuse!*

I have written this chapter after consultation with current and former learners and teachers in higher professional education, who have been involved with a wide range of academies and programmes. I have also spoken to experienced youth work practitioners employed in a wide range of settings. Over several years this amounts to close to a hundred people. I have tried as far as possible to include a cross section of views and contributions but it is fair to say that the overwhelming response was critical and reflective of dissatisfaction with current training practice, its theoretical credo and almost priestly class of academic proponents. Together with this I have drawn on my own personal experience of and in a number of institutions in the youth work sector over the last quarter of a century. I would like in particular to thank the following people who hail from across the professional broad prospect of youth work practice, education and training sectors;

Rosy Adraenssens
Zuber Ahmed
Penny Allen
Tricia Bowie-Phillips
Andrew Broughton
Barry Burke
Tania de St Croix
Stuart Dexter
Carol Farrell
Stephen Harrison
Jane Herbert
Darren Mulley
John Peaper
Mark Roberts

## WIND AND WORDS

Throughout the chapter I have inserted a diverse range of brief opinions about the nature of teachers and teaching both to stimulate and orientate thinking. I have also included quotes from *Inherit the Wind* by Jerome Lawrence and Robert E. Lee.

The play is a fictionalized retelling of the famous 1925 Scopes 'Monkey Trial', which resulted in John T. Scopes' conviction for teaching Charles Darwin's theory of evolution to a high school science class, contrary to a Tennessee state law that prohibited the teaching of biological evolution. The narrative provides a study of the struggle between literal interpretation of the Bible and secular science. The point that the play makes is that there may be no contradiction between science and religion, however by restricting focus on the letter, the literal interpretation of the text and not the spirit of religion, we create divisions for ourselves. It is a similar insistence of the adherence to form, the restriction of interpretation and the development of alternative practice that stymies differentiated teaching practice so logically (and perversely) destroying opportunities to accommodate the diverse learning styles and needs that are part of the richness students of youth work bring to the training context.

Most of the references from the play present the voice of Henry Drummond, the defending council for the fictionalised science teacher Bertram Cates, who functions as the mouthpiece for the play's authors Lawrence and Lee. Drummond fights for what he effectively sees as the moral imperative of humanity, to express that which marks us out in nature; our ability and drive to question and rationalise. As such he also argues for 'the right to be wrong.' At the same time Drummond seeks to spark a consciousness in townspeople of Hillsboro (the setting of the fictionalised trial) about narrow-minded fundamentalism and how this can thwart or even obliterate the pursuit of truth and thus cause us to inherit nothing but the wind (words without meaning).

A central intention of the playwrights was to criticize the then current state of McCarthyism or anti-Communist investigations of the House Committee on Un-American Activities (HCUA). Lawrence and Lee deployed the Scopes trial as the background for a drama that comments on and explores the threats to intellectual freedom presented by the anti-communist hysteria. In 1996 Lawrence commented in an interview that,

*We used the teaching of evolution as a parable, a metaphor for any kind of mind control...It's not about science versus religion. It's about the right to think.*

This, in essence, captures the trajectory and purpose of the following pages, set on the specific stage of higher professional education.

## JUSTIFYING DIFFERENTIATION

A Director of Quality with the London Central Learning and Skills Council (LSC) told me;

*Differentiated teaching and learning begins with and is informed by the initial assessment of learner skills, knowledge and abilities and enables teachers to plan for, often alongside learners, and provide suitable support that will effectively enable learners to achieve learning outcomes. Such approaches are equally applicable to all learners while they provide teachers with the means to clearly identify potential extension or learning support activities. This of course is just as appropriate at the higher levels of educational engagement as at any other stage.*

However, it would be remiss of me not to acknowledge my own position on differentiated learning and teaching, much of which has been formulated over the last few years in the pursuit of research. For Clough and Nutbrown (2002),

*...research which did not express a more or less distinct perspective on the world would not be research at all; it would have the status of a telephone directory where data are listed without analysis* (p. 10).

Personal, political and practice motivations for research are also relevant;

*...it is important not only to acknowledge these influences rather than affecting a spurious neutrality about social issues, but also to be open with one's readers about where one stands.* (Fairclough 2001, p. 4).

I have found that an honest, open, relatively transparent approach to teaching and learning in the higher education in particular is helpful in that it sets a stage for argument and so analysis. A youth worker practicing in East London commented,

*I have been on the most crap training courses where the teacher says they are flexible but refuses to teach at all, just wanting everyone to 'share their experiences' in some fluffy, non-judgemental way that doesn't add meaning to anything; the kind of person who sits and nods, and answers every question with another question but who is hardly ever willing to contribute themselves. I can't be doing with that! What does that kind of teacher think they actually add that we couldn't do without them? We'd spent time and money on this. Even if they refuse to teach, at least they may as well join in, seeing as they are there anyway.*

What this practitioner is asking for is really relatively straightforward dialectical science teaching at root; 'I have found this in that light of doing this to that – what do you think?' Unfortunately her experience has been something like 'we are all right (correct) in our different ways'. Apart from this leaving little to question (the basic building block of the educational process) in this situation the teacher by definition has nothing to add that is more pertinent than the most inexperienced, naïve or uninformed person in the group; all that righteously exists is opinion.

We instinctively know this deifying of neutrality, be it in the realm of research or teaching, to be a sort of anti-knowledge approach. The researcher comes to their subject with a bias and this is, in the best of worlds, brought to the awareness of the reader as the foundations of necessary critique.

In youth work training however it is not unusual for neutrality to be presented as a taken. In such circumstances, without any real knowledge of those seeking to be taught, there is an assumption that we are all as smart, imaginative and socially articulate as one another (but in mysteriously 'different ways') about everything to be discussed and everything said is, just because it has been said, relevant. But if this were the case we could also just reverse the supposition and claim that everyone involved was equally ignorant and whatever was said by anyone was uniformly irrelevant. Both perspectives are equally valid as each set of presumptions are unsupported by any discernable effort to establish the relative intellectual, social etc. capacities of the individuals taking part in the teaching process or their practical grasp of pertinent issues.

It has become something of a cliché in youth work training that each person involved has something, a contribution to make. This is perhaps true, but that 'something' is always going to be relatively positive or negative, helpful or obstructive, informed or uninformed. People come to potential learning situations with all sorts of hopes, concerns, motivations and ambitions, which they are more or less aware of. The contribution of some might be to make no contribution; people can be (often quite justifiably) defensive, protective, cautious or obstinate as much as they can be open, expressive, honest and engaged. An aspect of group life in general is that no one enters any collective entirely neutral, disengaged from their values, beliefs, fears, ambitions, hopes, resentments, passions, desires, prejudices and enthusiasms. It is these considerations that make being with groups interesting, enlightening and sometimes a little risky.

As such, objectively, the best one might draw from the neutral stance is that it involved people doing not much more than pooling anecdotes in trade for the palliative comfort of the clear fiction that this constitutes, of itself, understanding and/or knowledge. However, it is the combining of our individual bias and our collective predispositions that provide the potential for dialectical discourse; the bringing of new ideas into the world.

Freire (1998) makes it clear that so-called neutral education is in actuality the antithesis of dispassion, in fact suggesting the claim for impartiality is in practice propaganda as it,

*...uses the classroom to inculcate in the students political attitudes and practices, as if it were possible to exist as a human being in the world and at the same time be neutral* (p. 90).

As such, I admit to my advocacy (although of a questioning variety) of differentiated practice. My own approach to the area, arises out of my experience of youth work and has been developed during more than 20 years of teaching and training youth workers. This was initially informed by early years teaching and the ideas of Pestalozzi and Fröbel. However the literature on differentiated approaches is vast, some recent and intriguing examples include Deco, Fairchild and Follet (2007) Tomlinson, Brimijoin, and Narvaez (2008), Dodge (2006)

> *The best teachers teach from the heart, not from the book. A teacher's purpose is not to create students in their own image, but to develop students who can create their own image. Teaching should be full of ideas instead of stuffed with facts.* – Unknown

> *I hate the way that the 14–19 vocational courses are being shoved towards the 'non-academic' learners, who are being denied the opportunity of acquiring beautiful knowledge for knowledge's sake. It all about 'Let's just make sure they get a job in bricklaying and don't become NEET'* – Youth Worker, Essex

Over the last few years, working in the context of higher professional education, I have increasingly noticed what feels like a growing insistence (almost) on the part of teaching staff on following a standard range of teaching conventions and have dealt with a growing resistance to looking at alternative pedagogic vocabulary and teaching techniques. At the same time, I have found students surprised, but also often relieved and enlivened, when they discover that they can take opportunities to find, what are for them, new ways of sharing and developing professional practice and learning. Rather than merely receiving ideas, questioning theory and building on their own insights.

Some time ago I spent an academic year working with a tutorial group that from the outset were keen to try to think about ways of presenting their practice in a different fashion to what had become for them (in their first year of undergraduate study) the usual, quite formalised, approach. The latter involved each student taking turns to present a particular example of their face-to-face work. This task was described in the student handbook as follows;

*Each student is required to present at least one presentation of practice at each level. This is a particular way of working that involves individual students in bringing a specific intervention or interaction involving them as workers, presenting it to the group and then exploring it as an aspect of practice.*

We looked at this together and the associated aims and advice on the organisation of the presentation. Having discussed this, the group debated how they might continue to adhere to the prescribed process, but allow for a more organic approach. This involved no schedule but an open, ad hoc agenda for presentation. This meant that while each tutorial session would involve at least one presentation, which might take the form of what had for the group become the conventional model of presentation, members would also be able to 'blend-in' their presentations with others, responding as and when motivated by another's presentation. I made it clear (as I do with all the groups I work with in this type of pursuit) that they would need to make sure they all presented otherwise I might have little to relate to when it came to writing the tutor's report, a function of which was to assure they had participated to a level congruent with required learning outcomes.

Over our time together, the group engendered a type of 'pass-the-baton' process of presentation. One member would start with consideration about an intervention and/or aspect (or aspects) of their practice. The narrative would then be embellished or taken up by another, picking up on a trail of logic or responding to a particular or general motivation. This happened in a number of ways. It might start by questioning the presenter or confirming their position with a similar (or otherwise) example of practice. On occasion one piece of presented practice remained the focus of the entire session, at other times, over the hour or so we were together, the metaphoric 'baton' was carried by every member of the group at least once and by some several times. The 'baton' was held at points for a relatively short, although profound moment, wherein the group were caused to ponder or protest. Occasionally one person might have been stimulated to deliver a lengthy oration that could have been inspirational but at least once provided a sort of a sermon that had an anaesthetising effect. However, overall the process was far more energised and in terms of the group's engagement, enthusiastic than most tutorial groups I had experienced in previous years.

This sort of interaction is demonstrated by the depiction of the interaction between Oliver Kilbourn, George Brown, Harry Wilson, Jimmy Floyd and a 'Young Lad' in Lee Hall's play *The Pitmen Painters* (2008, p. 72–75). These men lived and worked (although the 'Young Lad is unemployed) in a North Eastern Pit Village in the 1930s. The play is based on a true story about working class people discovering and producing art together, although having minimal education and opportunity. You will see how they chip in and out of the description of their collective experience, moving from the particular (Van Gogh's *Sun Flowers*) to the general (their understanding of art and what art is for them). There is a movement from the appreciation of creativity to being creative and on to developing a notion of what creativity is and its impact on the individual via the generation of insight though knowledge and reasoning out of which understanding might, can and does emerge. In the process they state their point of view and position and the reader gets a sense of each personal and unique perspective adding to the whole.

The discourse (that evolves into a dialectic) is not dominated by anyone but, like their experience of art, is developed as a series of shared insights, reinforced and expanded upon in the making. Power, economics, spirituality, values, the nature of energy and inspiration (as well as other considerations) are broached. You might be able to sense the energy and even wonder that evolves within what appears to be a process of enlightenment that emerges out of their consideration of their practice as artists.

**Oliver** When we saw Van Gough. Something happened.

**George** we became a group.

**Oliver** Because we saw art was not about the privileged.

**George** It wasn't about money.

**Harry** Or doing things a right or wrong way.

**George** Art was a gift -

**Oliver** – a vision –

**Jimmy** - we all have, one way or another.

**Oliver** It was about living.

**George** Some of us to paint.

**Jimmy** Others of us to look, and see.

**Young Lad** Art was about how you live your life.

**Oliver** And is to be cherished.

**Harry** And it is to be shared. Art doesn't really belong to anybody.

**Jimmy** Not the artist.

**Harry** Or the owner.

**Jimmy** Or the people who look at it.

**Oliver** Real art is something shared –

**Harry** - power that's shared.

**Young Lad** Real art belongs to everyone

**Harry** And when we looked at a picture –

**Oliver** – we felt a force. That force that flowed through the flower – flowed through us.

**George** You could actually feel it.

**Jimmy** Something he had done.

**George** We were feeling it, as one.

**Harry** You might call it spirituality -

**Oliver** – or religion or creativity or energy –

**Harry** – or inspiration.

**Oliver** Yes.

**George** And we could feel it.

**Oliver** 'Cos he'd captured that energy –

**Young Lad** – of being alive.

**Oliver** It was an inspiration -

**Harry** – and that's what 'inspired' means. Doesn't it?

**Oliver** Breathing life.

**George** When yer inspired – it means seeing clearly how to capture that energy.

**Jimmy** It means knaaing what to de. (*knowing what to do*)

**Oliver** You see what is there. And you see what is possible.

**Jimmy** You can take one set of things –

**George** – some board, some paint, whatever.

**Jimmy** You can take this one set of things –

**Oliver** – and you can make them something else.

**Harry** Whatever your circumstances -

**Young Lad** – rich or poor.

**Jimmy** And you make them something else.

**Oliver** This is what art shows you.

**George** No matter how hard or how easy.

**Oliver** You can take things.

**George** And transform them.

**Harry** You don't have to put up with what you're given.

**Jimmy** And not just into anything.

**George** You can transform things and make something beautiful –

**Jimmy** - something profound.

**George** You can make something –

**Jimmy** – that's the work of art –

**Harry** – that you can change things.

**Oliver** And you can overcome whatever you need to overcome.

**Harry** No matter who you are, where you come from.

**Oliver** You need a brush –

**Jimmy** – or whatever –

**Oliver** – canvas or a bit of old card –

**Young Lad** – and change things.

**Harry** And that is what is important about art.

**Jimmy** You take one thing –

**George** and you make one thing into another –

**Oliver** – and you transform – who you are.

A youth worker in south-east England said of the above;

*This puts me in mind of the forum theatre stuff developed by Augusto Boal. Many practitioners would be scared to death at the thought of applying this approach, because it is hard to assess and with the constraints of the National Curriculum (Youth Service Curriculum) and OfSTED, it's hard to quantify - by their standards.*

As you might become conscious as you follow the pitmen's exploration, the openness and interactivity of the discourse appears to motivate thought and expression in a way that closely controlled turn taking might not. Moreover, what we know of creativity inclines us to understand that it is less probable to arise out of regimentation than relatively free moving expression, the latter being the more likely cradle of innovation and the former a provocation for resistance.

It is probably true that it would be idyllic (and probably false) to say this kind of potential exists in every group or in any group all of the time, it certainly doesn't amongst the pitmen throughout the course of the play. Dissention is at least as likely as cooperation, but this doesn't really matter as new lines of thought can and perhaps should be ploughed (the dialectic) and this maybe relies on the precursors of disagreement, argument and even conflict.

Some, maybe many of the interactions will end in cul-de-sacs or at least leave a few people frustrated temporarily, but this might be just the sort of motivation needed for further investigation.

Looking at the above, an ex-youth worker (as if such a thing existed) now a Chief Executive of 'Mind' reflected

*This analysis resonated with me. Like education art has become a commodity. I speak from my own experience of the music industry here; where music, as with football, involves obscene sums of money and multi-national companies and has subsequently become 'artless'. The observation that this type of group process would not always be successful and could lead to 'cul de sacs' is key here – cul de sacs would mean failure and failure is not allowed in educational practice (even if authorities insist what doesn't work is as important as what does – this is a lie. Practitioners merely get better at fabricating successes).*

If we are to engage with theory we might start by grasping that any particular idea cannot be understood as generically relevant or applicable regardless of cultural setting, time and place. As professionals, acting with appropriate discernment and regard for the unique character of our clientele in any given situation, we need to demonstrate the ability to usefully deploy ideas. But *using* theory is not just the mechanistic/instrumental adoption of the same – it means adapting, developing and perhaps sometimes rejecting elements or the whole of a body of received wisdom. If we fail to assert ourselves on theory any set of notions can evolve into dogma and/or professional credo (a'la informal education?). At that point we at risk effectively making ourselves the tool of prescribed ideology and thus subjecting those we work with to unmediated domination of the same. Like the pitmen, to gain anything close to an authentic understanding of how we might use ideas we need to apply our own perspective to them. Mostly anyone can follow rules, it is the professional role, via the application of professional judgement, to develop and shift regulation, instruction and received wisdom in order that they might serve rather than stifle the expression of those we work with, for and amongst.

## CURIOSITY

A while ago I met with the Canadian Olympic Gold Medalist Bobsleigher of 1964, Vic Emery (in connection with a book that I was writing) at the Berkley Hotel, London. Vic has had a fascinating life but he made one statement that made me think particularly hard;

*The difference between a winner and a loser is curiosity...but someone or something has to arouse your curiosity and one good way to do that is to present someone with the unexpected...something that for whatever reason draws them in.*

On the underground journey home I wondered why this particular bit of the chat kept coming back to me. I got to thinking how predictable patterns of teaching can dull the spark of learning and of an underlying principle (one of many) of traditional university scholarship.

*Plures sentential, plures mores* (many thoughts, many ways).

It is arguable if original thinking/ideas hardly ever arise out of an environment that lacks the fire of the kind of dissatisfaction that rouses curiosity. A youth worker in Brentwood, west Essex recalled;

*When I was at college I would sometimes go along to a particular tutor's classes and end up wanting to open a vein - but in a good way and I love that person for that! Although I would like to be taught by Will Self or the lovely Alan Bennett with tea and macaroons but learning (if it is learning) is not always comfortable.*

> *With all respect to the bench, I hold that the right to think is very much on trail! It is fearfully in danger in the proceedings of this court...A thinking man! And he is threatened with fine and imprisonment because he chooses to speak what he thinks* – Drummond, Lawrence, J., Lee, R.E. (1951) *Inherit the Wind* Ballantine, Act 2, Scene II (p. 72)
>
> *Then why did God plague us with the power to think? Mr Brady, why do you deny the one faculty, which lifts man above other creatures on the earth: the power of his brain to reason. What other merit have we?* – Drummond, Lawrence, J., Lee, R.E. (1951) *Inherit the Wind* Ballantine, Act 2, Scene II (p. 93)

However, at the same time, learners need to feel their investment in their education is credible and as such we need to be curious about them in the context of their studies. An experienced youth worker translating this to their own practice argued;

*If you just go on about what needs to be done or what you have done the young person can get lost in this, submerged and subordinated by the primacy of the practitioner's experience.*

The need to put the learner at the centre of teaching practice was reiterated by a community worker and manager of a south London Travellers Action Group however, as she pointed out, this requires levels of talent and dedication;

*I am one of those non-traditional learners that responds really well to differentiated techniques however, I know that some people learn better in what might be called traditional ways. The fact of the matter is though that a lot of teachers either lack the skill or fail to commit the necessary energy to their work. Or they may just never have developed sufficient insight to infuse those they work with.*

An individual involved in the training and education of youth workers framed the challenge;

*I think the question is how to catch the attention of those who lack imagination and courage, who find themselves more likely to encourage the students to consult the handbook as their standard riposte to a potential opening for critical enquiry.*

15

*My colleague and I have for the last two years been trying to square the circle, or circle the parallelogram, of prescribed learning programmes within our teaching. I think we have made some headway but we both recognise the role disposition and character etc. have in the equation and have come to the tentative conclusion these cannot be legislated for.*

> *The best teacher is the one who suggests rather than dogmatizes, and inspires his/her listener with the wish to teach themselves.* - Edward Bulwer-Lytton

## INNOVATION

The tutor group (referred to above) in evaluating our time together at the end of the year referred to their enjoyment and linked their learning to this feeling. But the conversation became more involved when we began to ask where the enjoyment might have come from. There were (as might be expected) a number of conclusions; 'We felt more in control', 'I felt more free to take things along another path so you could learn more' etc. However, all agreed the excitement and the pleasure evoked came from personal and group innovation. They had spent their first year at University working in what they regarded as a very formalised and predictable way. Some had experienced quite similar processes in their practice situation and in other areas of their study. As such, what they saw as 'their way' had given them not only a feeling of personal ownership of the learning situation and process, it had engendered the sense of responsibility and freedom that would logically accompany such a ethos. The experience of developing differentiated learning and teaching had taken them out of what they had identified as a sort of 'tram-line' of learning and provided them (or they had provided themselves) with the possibility to enhance their experience via their own innovative action.

Connected to this, a youth working in Surry who is involved in organising home-teaching reflected;

*To offer some potential and excitement when teaching a group is a bit like getting a new pair of trainers (the old ones are well comfy but look dated and/or are falling apart). It can produce a unique experience for a group who is willing to go beyond the prescribed model, but they would probably be pretty cohesive from the start, been together long enough to become frustrated with the 'old model'. However, I remember the discussions with a group I was studying with about us being quite a 'disparate' bunch whose work (writing/reading) never seemed to reflect being a group on the same course and we did work in fairly differentiated ways.*

> *Good teaching is one-fourth preparation and three-fourths theatre.* - Gail Godwin

> *The art of teaching is the art of assisting discovery.* - Mark Van Doren

I have worked with other tutor groups on and off in this way since the experience considered above. Of course some groups just start the academic year on auto-pilot, doing what they have always done – which of course has been okay by me. But most learners involved in these groups have consistently managed to develop discourse and dialectical interactions relating to their practice, some more than others of course. And groups have usually produced favourable and even a few enthusiastic responses to the learning processes they have played a part in creating, although there have been aspects of my own response that I have reviewed, particularly at moments and times when groups have become bogged down in one issue or allow a single member to consistently take responsibility for the work, sometimes being accused of dominating[2].

In retrospect, people (including me) taking up the differentiated route seemed to work harder than those had stayed strictly within the parameters of what was understood as convention. In the main, folk walked away, by their own insinuation, more informed in terms of the purpose of achieving set outcomes and clearer about the means and objectives of exploring, considering and discussing practice.

Looking at this point with a youth worker who has recently undertaken some teaching practice produced some interesting ideas;

*What stops people teaching 'flexibly' or improvising? There is the fear of failure and chaos and of drifting so far from the point it's hard to get back. I do think it takes a certain confidence to move away from the safety of a structure. I guess I don't want to cheat people. I don't want them to have a worthless experience. I am not yet a good teacher so I can't rely on skill to get me through!*

*But why start with a structure all the time? Why not learn to improvise from the start as I have with youth work? Let the structure emerge out of the task occasionally?*

> *A teacher who is attempting to teach without inspiring the pupil with a desire to learn is hammering on cold iron.* - Horace Mann

A Service Development and Commissioning Officer for Youth, working in the North West of England reflected;

*I think sometimes students come with a preconceived idea of what learning is about and what tutors or teachers should do. This is often based on past experience. I remember being at a College Residential in my first year as an undergraduate. Students were frustrated by the lack of teaching by tutors when they facilitated groups, expecting to be lectured to or challenged whereas the tutor just listened to the group talk – some tutors didn't even speak – it was quite un-nerving for quite a few people.*

*I think the key is to inspire the learner and get them excited about wanting to know more. That is what worked for me (as a student).*

Looking back on this practice with the learning group both my intellect and instinct tell me that in seeking to achieve consistency of outcome and hopefully the achievement of excellence, it appears that working with learners to identify the most helpful means and techniques to facilitate their learning is beneficial. This would be regarded as best practice within the 'third level'[3] sector but also across the horizon of education. At the same time such efforts seem to make sense in terms of developing a diversity of method and offer flexible approaches, responsive to learning needs and outcome requirements.

Accomplishing this balance is part of university tradition[4] and is funda-mental in the pursuit of distinctive professional activity that is associated with the generation of 'best practice'; we need to seek out distinguished methods and styles more than merely look to replicate teaching procedures and tactics for little reason beyond the felt need for regimentation. Thinking about innovation with learners and not for them via formulaic procedures, diverts us away from the predictable and humdrum and towards discovery and originality, something that they can habituate, making their own practice novel and as such distinctive. Discussing this with youth workers provoked a number of confirmatory responses, perhaps best represented by the following;

*Here, here!! Kids get enough of that when they're at work!!!!*

And

*Functionality verses creativity, knowledge verses imagination . . .it's clear where ingenuity is inspired...the means of making the kind of judgements required of youth workers.*

> *The teacher who is indeed wise does not bid you to enter the house of his wisdom but rather leads you to the threshold of your mind.* - Kahlil Gibran

## A PROCRUSTEAN BED

Uniform (non-differentiated) teaching and learning methods often take the form of a set of prescribed instruments implemented through a premeditated didactic attitude. These largely undifferentiated strategies are frequently applied within institutionally defined styles and approaches. They might be quite dogmatic or premised on a suite of fairly generic guidelines that are, nevertheless, suggestive of a prescriptive routine.

When I put this to one long-time youth worker they responded,

*Too right – all students are expected to fit and lay on a procrustean bed to learn*

A uniform method is applied from 'above', which implies that learners must 'reach up' to it. See below; the thick black line dissecting the graph horizontally is the uniform method that students are required to strain to touch .

### Prescriptive/Uniform Method

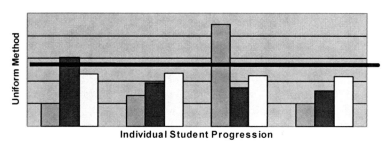

Individual Student Progression

Uniform methods are useful when variables, such as where the learner 'is at', their ability and favoured learning styles are unknown (such information is normally gained via interview, assessment etc.). Such methods and attitudes might also have a place in delivery to groups who are at approximately the same place intellectually, socially and in terms of readiness for learning. They may also be instrumentally practical if teaching staff are inexperienced, lack time, skill or confidence, although learner resistance to uniformity and/or the disorientation of groups of learners with relatively heterogeneous learning preferences, experiences of education or capability might undermine the confidence of less experienced/skilled teachers.

The extent to which uniform methods are

a) uninformed by knowledge of the learner

   and

b) are delivered largely unmediated by the learner (the learner merely reacts to the institutional model put in place by the teacher) dictates the level to which the uniform method is contrary to the custom and practice of equal opportunity. This is because the scope for equal access to learning is being dictated by the level at which learning is pitched rather than consideration of learner's needs, capacity, potential, ability, background, learning history, culture or strengths.

After discussing the above with an experienced youth worker (who told me *I took this exercise as a challenge, a chance to do something other than monitoring returns and funding applications!*) they responded;

*This expresses what I have always felt and known. This makes the case for ensuring that practitioners needing to use flexible teaching methodologies are well trained, considered and reflective. I can relate to this in my own practice and the practice of those I work alongside. One needs a well defined sense of self to let go and teach flexibly rather than rely on the 'safe' systems. Failure is always a possibility when one dares to practice according to a flexible methodology! But then John Dewy argued that failure is instructive ahd that the person who really thinks learns at least as much from their failures as they do from success.*

> *Excellent and advanced skills teachers should have a critical under-standing of the most effective teaching, learning and behaviour management strategies, including how to select and use approaches that personalise learning to provide opportunities for all learners to achieve their potential. (Training Development Agency (2007) in Cambridge Primary review* http://www.primaryreview.org.uk/Downloads/Finalreport/CPR-booklet_low-res.pdf p.34)

Uniform method is not effective in terms of equality or consistency of outcome as it is limited in its function to respond to individual learner needs because in its hardest incarnation it is a 'one size fits all model' - it has been designed to be followed rather than be tailored to a particular group and/or unique personal learning requirements/tastes/needs. In that respect, according to the level that standardised teaching responses might be said to be 'prejudging' their background and disposition as learners, neglecting sensitivity to their individual and collective experience, their actual and potential needs, it is based on a simplistic form of prejudice and is undemocratic.

Discussing this with a Senior Service Manager in youth and community work field stimulated the following response;

*For many learners their experience has been limited mostly to being told what to do, how to do it and to be assessed and graded though exams and/or forms of routine assessment. This has also been prolific in training for teachers and the delivery of the national curriculum. It leaves little room to encourage thinking outside of that very formal thinking, but this seems to be out of step with current trends in other areas. As the teaching becomes more structured there is a need for more flexibility in thinking and learning.*

*Companies like Google actively encourage their staff to develop new programs, and give them time during their working day to work on their own projects. This positively encourages innovation and is in contrast to Apple who strictly monitor their staff to the point of videoing them at work; they are also very closed and secretive about their operations.*

*The Open University is currently offering lectures to down load for your iPod/I phone. One of the philosophy lectures is being down loaded 5,000 times per week. The problem is that education like this is often not recognised unless it's in the form of some type of exam or proof of learning. I'm sure it will not be long before the 'i-degree' is born with formalised lectures, down loaded via the Apple store.*

> *Don't try to fix the students, fix ourselves first...When our students fail, we, as teachers, too, have failed.* - Marva Collins

## REFORMING THE FORMULATED

Differentiated (flexible) methods are essentially responsive in character. They can be applied in a range of learning situations and deployed to achieve required learning outcomes by way of responding to diversity of needs/requirements.

## Flexible/Responsive Method

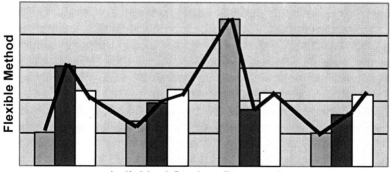

**Individual Student Progression**

Flexible methods should enhance institutional aims and approaches (if they depart from the same, they might be thought to have degenerated into confusion and in loss of direction).

Gravitating more towards innovative interpretation of curriculum rather than predictable routine, flexible methods take into consideration where the learner 'is at'; their ability, history and favoured learning styles (understood via focused discourse and continuous assessment).

In the above graph the thick line representing receptive teaching meanders across the page, address and responding to the situation of each learner; teaching method reaches towards learner requirements in response to where they are in terms of their learning development and trajectory.

Talking to a school based youth worker about this they asked;

*Is it time to acknowledge the current 'personalised learning' agenda in formal, secondary education?*

Flexible methods of teaching and learning are well suited to learners from diverse intellectual and social backgrounds, with distinct experiences of education and varying levels of readiness for learning. As one long term professional pointed out however, many are voting with their feet (or fingers) for more 'chaotic' forms of interactive learning;

*Internet forums encourage people to share and to learn from each other and form communities of collaborative, dialectical knowledge rather than from a single, particular source*

| |
|---|
| *The object of teaching is to enable people to get along without their teacher.* - Elbert Hubbard |
| *A teacher should have maximal authority, and minimal power.* <br> Thomas Szasz |

The delivery of flexible methods usually demand a relatively high level of teacher engagement and adaptability. Unpredictability is a consequence of flexible methodology and as such teachers need to constantly maintain and generate focus, imagination, skill and confidence while being able to harness, motivate and propagate the same in the learners with whom they engender differentiated teaching and learning practice.

Flexible methodology relies on movement towards learners and their inclusion/participation in developing practice and achieving outcomes. This involves 'reaching out' to learners that in response motivates learners reaching out to teach teachers about themselves and their world, invaluable information through which differentiated methods might evolve into a pattern of delivery and content most useful to the learners concerned. This makes teaching a more complex task but paradoxically perhaps a much more joyful and fulfilling experience, wherein both the teacher and the learner grow together, often interchanging roles.

Flexible methods are informed and shaped by knowledge of the learner and are delivered largely in collaboration with them (the learner is proactive in their own learning, creating their own path towards required outcomes). This does not preclude the teacher in any way, nor does it detract from their responsibility to teach. It does not render what is taught neutral or unhelpfully subjective, as the inclusion and consideration of learners does not set the teaching agenda or what is to be taught but does informs how learning is delivered, enrichening, animating and enlivening the means and context of education.

As such, flexible methods are in harmony with the custom and practice of equal opportunity. At the same time they can be effective in terms of equality and/or consistency of outcome, as flexible methods respond to individual learner needs within the framework of required outcomes; they are developed with consideration for a particular group and bring unique personal learning requirements/tastes/needs/biographies to the fore.

Overall, flexible methodology assumes that learners have the potential to play a part in identifying their own learning needs, developing their learning repertoire and distinguishing their own learning routes towards the achievement of required outcomes.

A colleague in higher education commented

*I wonder how some of the ideas here might connect with Vygotsky's thinking in terms of 'proximal zone of development' which for me at least seems to suggest learning occurs at the boundary of experience and understanding. The learner and teacher must be able to meet at this boundary and travel beyond it in order for learning to take place. However this process must be informed by a reasonable accurate (differentiated?) understanding of where the learner is at and the teachers capacity to connect with and provide a 'scaffold' for learning.*

At this point we shared a memory (that each of us had from the same place but different times);

*I was always more impressed by the scaffolding used in construction in Hong Kong. It was made form Bamboo rather than the galvanised steel we are accustomed to seeing in the west. Whilst the Bamboo looks a bit shaky it did the job, it flexed in the wind whilst giving the structure and support needed. Galvanised scaffolding, like many approaches to teaching, seems rigid and inflexible in comparison.*

> *The true teacher defends their pupils against his/her own personal influence. S/he inspires self-distrust. S/he guides their eyes from him/herself to the spirit that quickens him/her. S/he will have no disciple.* - Amos Bronson Alcott

### LOSS OF TRAJECTORY

Something of an occupational hazard of developing the boundaries of method is departure from or loss of trajectory towards the designated purpose and/or required programme outcomes. If this happens teaching might be understood to have defeated something of its own purpose in terms of institutional contracts with learners.

The lesson or learning session might be understood as a balloon that can be expanded by the learning/teaching methods used in it. As it inflates the balloon takes up more space (in consciousness say) making it a more notable (distinguishable) on the horizon of experience.

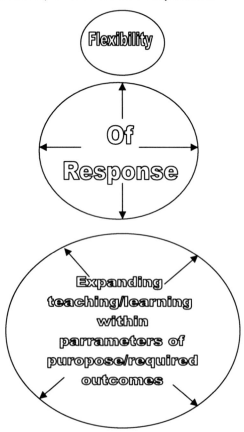

However, pushing the boundaries too far can result in deflection from purpose and losing sight of outcomes. Metaphorically this 'poor boundary maintenance' causes the teaching/learning balloon to burst; the point of the lesson or session is lost as learning objectives dissipate into a chaotic flux.

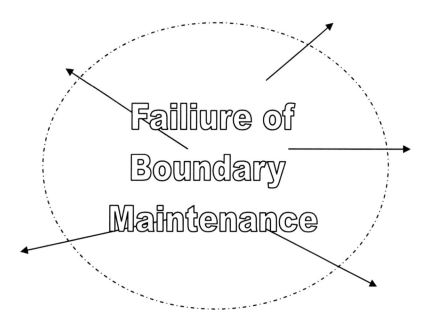

This can be an unpleasant experience for the teacher and that can demotivate learners as they fail to maintain their learning orientation. As such, in the aftermath of a collapse of the type depicted above it is not unusual for teachers and perhaps learners to look to retreat to more inflexible methodological regimen.

Indeed, it maybe that the fear a teacher might have of this scenario (the potential of innovative methods to result in a loss of what they might understand as 'control'), inhibits many from looking to develop and experiment with received/less differentiated methods. However, it doesn't need to 'all end in tears'. A youth worker in the south-west of England said of this model;

*I liked the analogy of the inflated balloon. I was facilitating a careers forum the other night in which the group were trying to work out the main objectives and function of the group. It got completely derailed and lost its focus only for the balloon to be burst right at the end. One woman said that the fact that things had gotten so off track made her realise what the group was not. This gave the whole group the opportunity to look from the outside in and realise their learning outcomes for that evening. Being lost or suddenly deflated gave them a real sharp focus and for me facilitating I had to endure what seemed like a life time of frustration without wanting to be directive or formal, only to find that they had found their own way in the end and seemed rather pleased with the outcome.*

But of course, we all need models and the feeling of 'allowance' to go where previously we may not have ventured. We might fall, but as long as the feeling exists that we can get up, the journey seems possible. Another experienced youth worker commented;

*I guess for me it is inspirational teachers that work with the students to encourage them to free their minds of rigid thinking that get the best out of their students. This can be done both in the formal and the informal setting but it is probably a two way thing. The student needs to develop the skills needed to think out of the box freely and openly; to question and not to always seek a definitive answer.*

## CONTROL

This said, some individuals, including some teachers, do have or can develop associations with power/self regard that might not be altogether facilitative of differentiated practice (Mark Mercer on 'weak/strong psychological egoism' is interesting in this respect[5]). In some cases any sharing of decision making is seen as a direct assault on position. This tendency can be mediated by self-awareness and the sharing of practice but might sometimes be associated with a lack of personal esteem, which will need both under-standing and perhaps other forms of personal development, training or in some cases individual counselling/therapy.

> *Most teachers have little control over school policy or curriculum or choice of texts or special placement of students, but most have a great deal of autonomy inside the classroom. To a degree shared by only a few other occupations...public education rests precariously on the skill and virtue of the people at the bottom of the institutional pyramid.* - Tracy Kidder

For all this, as can be understood from studying the results of the stern regulation of methods, the less teaching and learning are differentiated the more it is likely that learning groups will experience a greater level of incomprehension of purpose and subject, the progeny of which is relatively erratic and unsatisfactory achievement of outcomes and so dissatisfaction.

> *A good teacher is a master of simplification and an enemy of simplism.* - Louis A. Berman

> *...whenever you see something bright, shining, perfect-seeming – all gold, with purple spots – look behind the paint! And if it's a lie – show it up for what it really is!* – Drummond, Act 3, Scene I, Lawrence, J., Lee, R.E. (1951) *Inherit the Wind* Ballantine (p. 110)

It may be quite freeing to acknowledge that teachers do not control learning groups, just as prison officers do not control prisons and officers do not control armies. Prison, armies, schools, colleges and teaching/learning situations all function because of cooperation (between prisoners and prison officers, 'other rank' soldiers and officers and so on).

While a teacher has a role in guiding learners through course aims towards learning outcomes, unless learners collaborate in this enterprise, experience and history demonstrate that the time teachers and learners spend together will descend into a mutually destructive experience.

This being the case, boundary maintenance is not a control exercise it is more of a project that teachers and learners work on together. Using flexible methods, facilities like course aims and intended learning outcomes can act as compasses and maps, but the group, with the 'good offices' and counsel of the teacher, decides on the route to the designated destination. At any given instant anyone can make enquiry about trajectory, cadence or orientation. There is no time at which anyone may not ask questions like 'are we on the right route?' or declare 'I think we have got a bit lost'. In fact such statements are to be welcomed and taken seriously. If this is the case, a loss of direction every now and then is not in fact Armageddon, it is at worse 'I'm a-getting outa here!'

> *The mediocre teacher tells. The good teacher explains. The superior teacher demonstrates. The great teacher inspires.* - William Arthur Ward

## INFANTILIZING TYRANNY

Overly orchestrated learning is not only inherently undemocratic, in that at its most severe it responds to a form of bureaucratic tyranny[6], it effectively 'infantilizes'[7] learners while positioning the teacher in the role of parent. This invites justifiable forms of resistance as resentment is provoked, which can at points transmute into rejection of intransigent teaching regimes (sometimes called 'rebellion').

In relation to this an experienced a youth and drugs worker reflected;

*It is interesting how Primary school teaching has become quite progressive over the last 10 years, using play, colour, diversity and a relatively informal approach, similar to the Steiner philosophy. But when we reach the secondary school and young people hit puberty, issues of discipline and order reign in the classroom, we start to see the rise of the exclusions units. Those filtered out to the exclusions units are then encouraged to reach their learning outcomes via informal and relaxed means! What does this show?*

Another practitioner in the youth work field commented;

*This reminded me of Michael Bywater's 'Big Babies' where he suggests that modern culture (the media, advertising, et al) works to infantilise all of us - to arrest our development and keep us in a childish state to ensure we are compliant consumers. I think that there are parallels with the infantilization of learners, which ensures that learners are 'consumers' of training rather than people actively encouraged to think critically, challenge, explore and innovate.*

*Is there something about the true aim of education, perhaps, as Bourdieu suggests, education's task is to reproduce the dominant culture, not to challenge it.*

Instruction might sometimes be a precursor to education but it is no replacement for it. As far as we can tell orders and dictation (what one youth worker saw exemplified by *the government's apparent obsession with targets, league tables and the prediction of goals*) appear to erode rather than quicken enlightenment.

Improvisation alongside the practice of shared decision making in a context able to tolerate inventiveness, engendered by flexible thinking create a means and environment to hone and develop professional judgement. This makes sense if you ask yourself how simply following set teaching routines/instructions (the outcome of someone else's judgment) might enhance the independence of thought and empirical evidence gathering that the making of professional judgement is dependent upon.

After discussing this area with a particular youth worker she told me;

*...improvisation in anything is undermined by those who value banal outcomes... those who think it's preferable to have predictable mundane results, rather than uneven results which chop and change and are sometimes inspiring, maybe even exciting/mind blowing or perhaps sometimes disappointing but that's life.*

*I had two main teachers on my youth work diploma, one excellent, reliable, who always fulfilled the learning outcomes, but was mainly very structured, and I really liked and respected this teacher but it always boiled down to:*
- *teacher introduces subject*
- *handout*
- *exercise or discussion in small groups*
- *feedback to large group*
- *debate*

*Although it wasn't always in the same order, I for one often drifted off.*

*I was interested when I started reading youth work method books, called things like 'how to do fun activities about self esteem'. These books all followed the same method of discussion, small groups, blah blah - as if small groups equals democratic and participatory learning - Freire distilled and made impotent. What person in their free time would follow this for long without getting up and walking out? I have always been amazed these books keep getting published.*

*Anyway the other teacher at different times*

- *pissed me off*
- *criticised*
- *laughed*
- *went right off the point*

*Yes there was a danger of losing the focus on the learning objective and sometimes the session was a bit rubbish, but mostly it was amazing. I remember many of those sessions now, ten years later. All the best learning I have been involved with has been like this. I've been lucky to have a couple of great teachers who were flexible and varied what they did and were ready to fly off - but they were also rigorous, critical, not just nodding and going 'yeah, yeah, very interesting' which I think is lazy teaching.*

However, an Operations Manager in the *Groundwork* organisation argued;

*The political pressure exerted on practitioners can pervert the potential for good educational practice and educational activities that seek to educate.*

*I would argue that there is little place for 'Informal Education' in a 'market' driven by an overriding objective to tackle worklessness and to ensure all citizens contribute economically to society.*

> *What the teacher is, is more important than what s/he teaches.*
> - Karl Menninger

## CHARISMATIC RATHER THAN BUREAUCRATIC

Particularly in the field of youth work but also in other areas that encompass professional training and qualifications, 'molten' teaching methodologies and the kind of accommodating learning strategies that arise out of the same, are pertinent and appropriate. Uniformity of teaching practice, while not wholly inappropriate or straightforwardly signifying ineptitude cannot be seen as inherently apposite with respect to;
– equality of opportunity
– the development of professional judgement
– maximising the achievement of learning outcomes
– democratic learning environments
– expansion of learning horizons

   Indeed, in the field of youth work the place of inflexible pedagogic approaches might be limited in terms of their effects and applicability. As one long term practitioner argued;

*The modern obsession with 'systems' to ensure quality and best practice too often means the removal of the personality of the educator from the process of education. I believe that the polar opposite of this is the role I previously had as an educator and more recently as a manager of those who practice education. Weber's ideas about leadership styles have always resonated with me; I'm aware that I am a charismatic rather than bureaucratic manager. That's not to say that I'm a great bloke but that the success of my practice and those who I manage depends on my qualities (good memory, supportive, fair, inspiring, thought provoking) rather than my ability to adhere to systems and procedures (which I am really, really terrible at). I'm not saying either is right or wrong I'm just saying that's how I work.*

> *It's sad that we aren't all gifted with positive knowledge of Right and Wrong, Mr Brady* – Drummond, Act 2, Scene II, Lawrence, J., Lee, R.E. (1951) *Inherit the Wind* Ballantine (p. 93)

*I don't do absolutes. I am never sure. There is no black and white in my world; I live amongst a million shades of grey. It seems to me that to deliver non-differentiated teaching one needs to have a substantial degree of surety; you need to live life in black and white...that feels a bit...well boring.*

*Perhaps non-differentiated teaching is not only the professional norm but the dominant style. Maybe this is because contemporary education is delivered for the benefit of everyone apart from the learner; the systems are for the organisations and agencies not for the clients. This is one of the reasons that I find it hard to value NVQs* (National Vocational Qualifications); *they seem to be about getting to an end of a course rather than exploring ones view of the world. I have always been suspicious of youth workers who carry around a repertoire of responses to certain situations or behaviours. Surely our 'art' is to react appropriately and constructively in the moment, to the person, not to compute that 'they've said X so I'll say Y', 'A has happened, I'll do B.'*

> *A teacher is a compass that activates the magnets of curiosity, knowledge, and wisdom in the pupils.* - Ever Garrison

> *If the novice is deliberate, the advanced beginner insightful, the competent performer rational and the proficient performer intuitive, we might categorise the expert as being 'arational'. Expert teachers appear to act effortlessly, fluidly and instinctively, apparently without calculation, drawing on deep reserves of tacit knowledge rather than explicit rules and maxims.* (see Cambridge Primary Review; David Berliner (1994 and 2004) http://www.primaryreview.org.uk/Downloads/Finalreport/CPR-booklet_low-res.pdf p.34)

FORMAL/INFORMAL?

A former colleague in higher professional education wrote;

*The informal/formal split is such a red herring. So many students talk about being informal educators when really they are nothing of the sort and in today's field it is a completely irrelevant distinction.*

The perspective of this chapter might be understood as a formal versus informal education argument. Indeed, the attitudes and approaches that exemplify informal education could be taken to epitomize an ultimate incarnation of differentiated teaching and learning. This being the case, the foregoing analysis, in that it commends differentiated approaches in formal settings, at least serves to blur the supposed informal/formal dichotomy (if such a border might be said to exist).

However, after many years of reading undergraduate work in the field of youth work, I have found amongst the most reoccurring themes is the equation that more or less overtly states;

*Informal education = good*
*Formal education = bad*

This is probably a result of a combination of two influences in particular. Much of the literature and professional discourse concerning itself with informal education, more or less overtly, uses this simplistic equation to champion the techniques that propose informal education as a distinct approach. This combines with widespread negative experiences of school, seen by more strident propagators of informal education as the 'dark fount' and 'Minas Morgul' fortress of the prescriptive, inflexible, impersonal formal education.

Not only does this universally condemn teachers over time and place, it ignores the fact that most good teachers (those achieving outcomes while maintaining appropriate relationships with learners) use differentiated and informal methods (amongst the plethora of evidence of this presence see Rogers 2005, Ekwunife 1987, Merttens et.al. 2000, Green 2008).

For all this, as a youth worker dealing with professionals in training complained

*Students seem to be channelled into reinterpreting formal education as the antithesis of youth work! This seems more combative or about competitiveness than useful*

A practitioner in Essex commented;

*I am quite satisfied with the now much maligned 'chalk and talk' pedagogical style if the person talking floats my boat. I know Freire would dispute this willingness in me to be an 'empty vessel', and I don't just want to be filled up with stuff all the time, but it can be very exciting when someone sets off a spark of enlightenment or a crushing realisation.*

This demonstrates how differentiated learning can be mediated into formal settings and styles. However, anyone involved in teaching might ask how modern forms of so called 'formal education' might be possible without devoting a good deal of their teaching time to 'informal practice'.

At the same time, youth workers who by their own declaration deliver 'informal education' undertake this by using more or less sizable elements of what any disinterested observer would call 'formal practice' (instruction, advice and information giving, teaching etc.). As a youth worker pointed out to me,

*This was been developed further by the 'Transforming Youth Work' policy*

The person quoted at the outset of this section portrayed the possible consequences of supporting the formal/informal separation eloquently;

*We all do both and anyone who doesn't is quite ineffective. All good teachers teach formally and informally (as well as learn from their students). By continuing to effectively generate maintain a dichotomy between formal and informal education, we are, I think inadvertently creating a situation where teachers and youth workers are on a collision course because neither understands (or wants to understand) the other.*

A mixture of informal/formal methodology might be understood to be necessary in terms of diversity and facilitating differentiated practice, as a youth worker in the South West pointed out;

*I recall when I first experienced a particular lecturer's style. They were just saying what I was not able to express. I recall some of the class hated this person and simply would not hear what they had to say. But others, like myself, loved it and thrived on it (even though it was more challenging than other tutor styles).*

*So from a pedagogic perspective the formal approach has a place in a differentiating learning environment as it is valid for some people, as learning is easier for them in that style and perhaps for most people at some times (even Socrates inculcated his students with the love of truth). To offer both formal and informal responses is more within the spirit of equal opportunities. I think informal and formal education is at least interlinked (so close perhaps they are not really two entirely separate approaches). Perhaps some time would be better spent looking at how we might develop the colossal benefits of differentiated teaching methods (as they are increasingly a minority pursuit) than cogitating for inordinate amounts of time attempting to identify the supposed delineation between informal and formal education?*

This said, perhaps we are not being as insightful or as honest as we might be. A youth worker in North Eastern England provided an intriguing response;

*Do people in positions of authority really manage their subject with the consent of those they teach? Is the control implicit, implied and hidden so as to appear consensual? Isn't the fear of consequences the instrument by which control is exerted, however esoteric, subtle and amorphous those consequences are?*

*Informal = Bad*
*Formal = Worse*

*Ha Ha!*

These are valid and potentially devastating questions. Perhaps we need to stop pretending that the dichotomy between formal and informal is in any way concrete? Being at best an arbitrary and abstract demarcation that does little more than create confusion and a kind of prejudicial and therefore antagonistic oppositionalism, how long can we justify it as currency in educational debate? A youth worker with Gypsy and Traveller communities protested;

*When I was in college they would refer to informal education as if it were a profession in its own right, but there is no universally recognised professional body or set of parameters for informal education practice and you will see relatively few job advertisements asking specifically for an informal educator. In the main, informal education is a set of notional approaches, values and techniques applied in a number of settings, including schools and colleges, by a range of professionals. Contemporaneously it has been embraced by youth and community workers and folk delivering the wide range of services that fall under the title 'community education' (the nature of this practice varies from authority to authority and from nation to nation). But why keep on cracking on about it as if it were the saviour of human kind. 'Informal' usually means 'convert' anyway and how can 'covert education' be education? Covert education is indoctrination by way propaganda isn't it?*

Although this chapter has not centrally been an argument for informal over the formal education, one of the questions it begs is how one might differentiate the event horizon of 'informal' and 'formal' education given that I have argued that formal outcomes might best be achieved via interplay between informal attitudes, strategies and responses, together with references to formal procedures and tactics (this might probably be consistent with best practice examples in schools and youth agencies for example). At the same time, forms of formalised teaching and learning have their place in the pursuit of differentiated teaching and learning.

A youth worker with global experience (now and academic himself) argued;

*I think that something critical is missing (or too present) in the formal education of so called informal educators! I was trying to work with this when developing a course on Ethics and Values in Education. If, as Robin Barrow points out, we accept Richard Peters' assertion that the 'concept of education' has criteria built into it that renders the term as pointing to something 'worthwhile', we accept the informal and formal prefix becomes simply a matter of method rather than defining value.*

*Maybe I am deluded but I still cannot buy that the more informal a process is the greater value it has. The difference between the descriptive and normative distinctions concerning the use of the term education as offered by Paddy Walsh in Education and Meaning are really useful in this respect.*

Perhaps the last word in this section should go to the person who opened it;

*I get so fed up with students slagging off formal education and praising informal education. However, I do not think that it is necessarily the fault of their teachers, apart from the fact that institutions have created a model that has outlived its usefulness.*

Perhaps youth workers need now to deal with the growing consciousness that informal education as a distinctive practice is a fading paradigm. With this in mind we probably need begin to build professional frames of reference more in keeping with the social expectations of our role that in reality revolve around welfare and care functions (we have a legal duty of care and no legal duty to educate). This said, this does and should not disqualify us from continuing to uphold the educational values and responsibilities our profession has always encompassed and embraced.

> *In a child's power to master the multiplication table there is more sanctity than in all your shouted 'Amens'! 'Holy, Holies!' and 'Hosannahs!'An idea is a greater monument than a cathedral. And the advance of man's knowledge is more of a miracle than any sticks turned to snakes, or the parting of the waters! But are we now to halt the march of progress because Mr Brady frightens us with a fable? ...progress has never been a bargain, You've got to pay for it. Sometimes I think there's a man behind a counter who says, 'All right, you can have a telephone; but you'll have to give up privacy, the charm of distance. Madam, you may vote; but at a price; you lose the right to retreat behind a powder-puff or a petticoat. Mister, you may conquer the air; but the birds will lose their wonder, and the clouds will smell of gasoline!' Darwin moved us forward to a hilltop, where we could look back and see the way from which we came. But for this view, this insight, this knowledge, we must abandon our faith in the pleasant poetry of Genesis* – Drummond, Act 2; Scene II, Lawrence, J., Lee, R.E. (1951) *Inherit the Wind* Ballantine, (p. 93)

> *Who dares to teach must never cease to learn.* – John Cotton Dana

SHARING PRACTICE

Awareness of differentiated practice is vital to its development but also to short-circuit misinformation and misapprehension it is imperative that teaching experiences and practice direction are shared between colleagues. If one group of learners are energised and engaged in their learning with a particular teacher indulging in differentiated practice this can create jealousy and even anger in other groups, maybe frustrated by what they see as their more staid and/or routine experience. At the same time infantilized groups may generate activity according to how they have been treated and replicate social stereo-types of 'immature' behaviour. Gossip and anecdote mix rumour with fact; the 'other' group are just having a good time or are getting away with something that their peers are obliged to tolerate or suffer.

As the environment becomes more and more strewn with allegory, hearsay and competitive envy, so teacher colleagues immersed in their learning group's life can undergo a type of transference, colluding with their learners in the production of fables about the 'other' group, who laugh and debate loudly while their group stick dutifully and stoically to preset agenda and habitual, scheduled routine, heroically facing repetitious predict-tability and the accompanying tedium while maybe dealing with resistance given strength by the 'illicit' goings on in the 'other group'.

Of course enthusiasm and envy are bait to construction of laudable sagas of 'our group' and the generation of condemnatory prejudice of the 'other group' (that can become the 'rival camp'). Enquiry about the 'other group' with its teacher, or even listening to what the 'offending teacher' brings to both formal and informal conversations about the direction a group is taking, threatens to break the cosy spell of resentment, prejudice and discrimi-nation that Adorno et.al. (1994) demonstrated to be so assiduously protected by those once convinced by the seductively simplistic explanations of bigotry.

As such, no authentic exploration of practice occurs and as tension becomes inherent in the communal structure it evolves into a cultural norm. Official action, the recourse to law (or the nearest equivalent) appears to be the quickest and most acceptable muscle to stop the outrage. Scapegoats are created via expedient justification based on what tyranny of the majority view to be 'going on'. The dictatorship of the many over the few, the dominance of the conforming over the minority of the different, is camouflaged as a 'democratic perspective', while covert bullying is passed off the prevalence of justice.

Such situations can be to a great extent (if never wholly) avoided by way of a continuous curiosity about alternative forms of practice. This can be built into institutional training agenda, which can provide systematic forums for the sharing of practice or by routine classroom teaching inspection/ scrutiny. But while the former feels useful and the latter heavy handed and labour intensive outside the largest institutions, sharing practice and teaching experience might be better affected as a consistent element of institutional life by the promulgation of an informal and cultural ethos consistent with a 'learning community' (*universitas magistrorum et scholarium*[8] – 'community of masters and scholars')

*To teach is to learn twice.* - Joseph Joubert, Pensées, 1842

STUDENT EVALUATION/ 'FEEDBACK'

> *Show me a shouter,*
> *And I'll show you an also-ran.*
> *A might-have been,*
> *An almost-was* – Hornbeck
>
> Act 3, Scene I, Lawrence, J., Lee, R.E. (1951) *Inherit the Wind* Ballantine (p. 122)

This last section might be seen to diminish the value student evaluation, but this would be to misunderstand the use and worth of the same. Structured learner feedback is valuable to a learning community, just like customer response is an indispensable device in achieving retail success. It is certainly congruent with the promotion of differentiated teaching and learning. However, while a dentist must, if they are to remain in practice for any length of time, do what they can to enhance their patient's experience of treatment, it would be a mistake to look to these same people for advice on the intricacies (or rudiments) of the performance of root canal procedures or expect them to pursue their own research on the most up to date literature relating to the Lactobacillus bacteria so as to be expert in the dental response to the same.

Although it is interesting, informative and probably advantageous for learners to share their experience of learning, the role of the learner is to learn, certainly to question but not to instruct their teachers what and how to teach, else what is the worth of teaching qualifications, training and experience or the value of validation and quality assurance procedures (although learner feedback might be part of the latter)?

At the same time it is the role of the teacher to teach, respond to and learn from those they teach, how their teaching methods are experienced and alongside the achievement (or otherwise) of learning outcomes assess their own, their peers and their institution's performance.

One experienced youth work trainer argued;

*I think the issue of evaluation is really more than just tricky, it has the potential to absolutely corrupt the teaching process and relationship. If I piss a student off by pointing to a version of the truth that does not fit with their own and has the means to wake them from their cosy slumber, the potential exists for the homogenised, undifferentiated evaluation form to seek to reek vengeance on my audacity. I have largely adopted the 'fuck it' approach to evaluation, but cannot help feeling somewhat corrupted, undermined by not having the right to reply. Poor me! Well not really, I refuse to be reduced and commit to having the conversation, this will end up with me being asked to leave somewhere at some point I am sure.*

> *I'm sorry if I offend you. But I don't swear just for the hell of it. You see, I figure language is a poor enough means of communication as it is. So we ought to use all the words we've got. Besides, there are damned few words that everybody understands* – Drummond, Act 1; Scene II, Lawrence, J., Lee, R.E. (1951) *Inherit the Wind* Ballantine (p. 51)

Unmediated learner responses can be considered and thoughtful, but they might also be a throw away comment based on a whim or a fatigued answer to another, what at the moment they are quizzed about their teacher's performance, seems like another unnecessary question. Answers might be an attempt at humour or irony, forms of blether or intrigue or premised on any number of factors, including personal performance, emotional sensibilities or sometimes an interest in eliciting a particular response from one member of staff via another learner or teacher to kindle scandal, drama or entertainment (perhaps following another predictable and hackneyed session).

Interpretations of the perceived or actual agenda of friendship groups, cliques, clubs, factions and schisms all have their effects. Family affinities, political allegiance, demographic positioning, class or cultural interpretations/interests/loyalties, fear, anxiety, boredom, competitiveness are just a few more examples amongst many other influences on opinion, judgement, comment and response. How can we extract the facts of the experience of the academy, sometimes over years, just from what a random representation of people say at a particular moment within the confines of the institutional context, given the cauldron of prejudice, beliefs, uncertainties, taste, attitudes, values, discrimination, insight and ignorance that humanity is embroiled in?

To draw attention to all this is not to depreciate the contribution of learner feedback, it is appreciation of individual behaviour in group situations and how humans deal with and interact in the collective and community context (foundation sociology).

This said, learning has to be understood as intimately connected to emotional responses. As one youth worker put it,

*The power of emotion is implicated in learning. Dopamine is the key neurotransmitter connected with pleasure but also learning, co-ordinating thoughts and memorizing. The greater the emotional state is often connected*

*with greatest recall. This stimuli in the learning environment was for me the driver of curiosity, whether it be by way of joy or anger. To a degree this indicated I think that there has to be a degree of performance in effective teaching to elicit a response and any response that is not emotional to some extent is merely a reflex.*

Learner response, like teacher input, is as such hardly ever neutral, detached or objective and like other polls quite capable of being used to scapegoat (be deployed to apportion blame for actual, imagined or feared disappointment) the unconventional and different. What it enables is the possibility of an indication on how teaching is perceived, how curriculum is received (or ignored) and used (or rejected). Responses to one subject or teacher need to be considered in the context of a whole course or programme, as the whole impacts of the view of the particular. At the same time it is necessary to take prevalent attitudes towards gender, sexuality, disability, age, class, ethnicity, race and culture into account; teachers like learners are and have been subjected to unjust assessments on the basis of such considerations.

Although learner feedback (like all comment or critique) might be evidential of something, it is not of itself necessarily proof of anything. Unless placed alongside a mutual interaction of convivial enquiry about and munificent dissemination of practice (interplay between curiosity and diffusion) it is limited in its use. However, if learner response is purposely segregated from everyday shared, genial, but serious analysis of and debate about practice, to be used as a tool of retribution, an expression of vitriol against the sin of diversity, at some quasi-judicial event or committee room show trial, it is corrupted, being made hardly discernable from a tissue of malicious gossip.

Experience seems to indicate the questions 'what did I learn', 'how did I learn', 'what was the quality of my learning and how did the teaching impact on the same' need a little more time than an end of course questionnaires might allow.

A Youth Work Training Programmes Coordinator in Wales related to an experience during his training some two decades earlier;

*I remember studying Social Theory. The tutor was not present for the first session, instead he had left a whole load of info in our pigeon holes about a painting by Hans Holbein the Younger, it was called 'The Ambassadors'. Our curiosity as students was fired in a number of ways:*

*Many of us wondered 'where is the tutor?' and became annoyed by the absence of the teacher. Some of us further wondered 'what on earth has this painting got to do with youth work?'*

*Some of us then saw the opportunity to pursue the line given. We organised ourselves and went to the National Gallery to see it. This was the first time I had gone to a gallery with the overt intention to view art! My perspective on the world was changed in a permanent way.*

*Some might see this in the 'Educating Rita' mode of education or even identify hints of 'Pygmalion'. I do not. I don't buy the condescending triumph over adversity crap and about class and education. What is critical to understanding what was at the heart of this learning process is the following:*

- *Stimulation. (Attention to environment)*
- *A desire to learn. (Inquiring Minds)*
- *The possibility for something to be truly learnt. (some form of worthwhile; knowledge, skill acquisition or adjustment in attitude)*
- *The capacity to imagine possibilities and pursue them.*

*Lectures on/encounters with the work of R.D Laing, Michel Foucault, Max Weber, Emile Durkheim, Ferdinand Tonnies, Erving Goffman, the list goes on, followed, but at a stretch I can remember them all. What is more I consider myself to have a poor memory! What is important to realise here is that I have over the years made and remade sense of these experiences. I'm not sure to what extent - to borrow from Vygotsky – the tutor provided 'scaffold' for my learning, my sense is that he did! And to what sense my proximity to the zone of development being encountered was critical, again I think it was! But I am convinced that some critical examination of this experience is worthwhile in terms of unpacking some of the undisclosed aspects of the narrative relating to that tutor's approach as a teacher and mine as a learner. As I am sure there are points of juncture and disjuncture that have or not been either identified, or understood as yet.*

*What I think is particularly interesting to reflect on here, is not just how the teaching methods were differentiated per' se but also how the learners responses were differentiated.*

> *Teachers are expected to reach unattainable goals with inadequate tools. The miracle is that at times they accomplish this impossible task.* - Haim G. Ginott

## PERSONALISING LEARNING

A retired trainer/academic in the field of youth work told me;

*I always feel that there is a tension between the concept of focusing on the individual learner and the group. What about sub-groups within learning groups? How can the teacher reconcile the learning needs of quite disparate individuals and groups? Youth work students come from such a wide background with totally different experiences and biographies that that tension is always going to be the biggest hurdle for any teacher in the field.*

Of course, the above position is true. But this diversity can be as much of a resource as an obstacle. People bringing such a range of experiences, influences and knowledge are literally a mine of information and potentially, the providers of a stimulating learning environment.

In 2004 'Personalised Learning' seemed to be the great hope for education in the UK; the faith that 'one size fits all' was seen as dead as the government devoted itself to forms of differentiated practice.

At the time of writing, more half a decade later, many teachers, learners and parents might not feel things have changed much – to quote the Pet Shop Boys 'they didn't quite succeed' (*It's a Sin*).

When the Commons select committee on Children asked what was happening with personalised learning, it called on Professor David Hargreaves, something of a force in New Labour's educational philosophy. In his book 'The Challenge for the Comprehensive School' (1982) he argues that

*...our present secondary-school system ... exerts on many pupils ... a destruction of their dignity which is so massive and so pervasive that few subsequently recover from it.*

This work has been read perhaps by more teachers than any book since published on the subject. Throughout the 1980s, Hargreaves was the most talked about educationist in Britain.

Hargreaves advised Estelle Morris when she was Education Secretary, has been a member of the Standards Task Force, and, for a short time, Chief Executive of the Qualifications and Curriculum Authority.

The committee on Children believed that Professor Hargreaves had for the previous four years been working on government ambitions around personalised learning, having produced a series of pamphlets (23 of them) devoted to the same.

However, 70 year old Hargreaves appeared if anything to be more of a critic than a supporter of personalised learning. He is critical of almost every aspect of Secondary education; from teacher authority to the role of heads including subjects, lessons, classrooms, testing and year groups, calling for 'system redesign' that includes learners being involved in
– creating the curriculum
– informing schools how to use information technology
– setting standards and learning objectives
– assessment of their own and one another's work
– working for appreciable amounts of time on collaborative projects

In the brave new world that Hargreaves proposes teachers become more like coaches or mentors, who rather than grade learner's work merely comment on it. Subject areas are transformed into 'essential learnings', for example thinking, communicating or social responsibility. Other areas ('competencies') include relating to others and managing information.

Hargreaves envisages that the school as part of a wider network, encompassing colleges and other schools (potentially youth facilities), on occasion parts or the whole of a department's work.

'Personalised learning' is part of this mix, however Hargreaves wants to see a process of 'personalising' education as 'personalised' education has been distorted by government who have used it 'as a clothesline on which to hang existing policies' but it is made inappropriate as it implies a finished product.

The momentum for personalising learning, for Hargreaves emanates from below by way of teachers and heads changing the process of secondary education.

In his prolific pamphleteering he has pointed to a plethora of grassroots innovation. He declares;

*We are not talking about a new model of schooling, handed down from above...The notion that there should be or can be a standard model is dead.*

According to Hargreaves;

*Now customers actively contribute to innovation. Producers seek people's ideas for improving something. It becomes a partnership between producer and consumer. That's the way schools will go.*

At the centre of Hargreaves's vision is 'student leadership' and collaborative projects that he believes should be 'co-constructed', involving learners in dealing with 'authentic' issues and situations. He contests;

*That's how you get people to learn, not by presenting them with a set of things they have to learn by heart. When I was an undergraduate at Cambridge, the statistics course was so boring. But when I needed to interpret the results of my own research project, statistics became relevant and useful.*

All this sounds extraordinary 'right on', but in fact it is promoting consumer choice in education. For all this, as he reported

*...all our conferences were sold out and I've never before met so many confident, risk-taking people*

But he is not confident that the state will back this enthusiasm;

*They say they're in favour of innovation, but it has to be innovation they approve of. It's as daft as the Department for Industry telling business where it can and cannot innovate.*

*You might say a Conservative government would be more supportive than a top-down Labour government, since their rhetoric is all about local power for headteachers. But I don't know. Labour talked the talk, but it didn't change the policies.*

As such, while there is intellectual, academic and grassroots support for the most radical differentiated teaching and learning from those steeped in the practice and theory of education there is a deeply reactive force that resists and obstructs 'authentic' change. This is something much more primeval than left or right wing philosophies, both of which in their seminal form would broadly support a move away from the unsuccessful and clearly moribund procedures of stark undifferentiated, undistinguished forms of teaching. Is this fear of a loss of control? Or is it more disturbingly the operation of a sadistic, self-destructive social tendency?

CONCLUSION

I am not here arguing for some insane form of academic anarchy. I reiterate the need to pursue institutional and organisational aims and policy objectives. If any principle driven difference exists in the heart or mind of learners or employees inside education, these need to be pursued and aired along appropriate lines of communication and authority and not enacted in some futile and meaningless way in the flouting of agreed procedures and required outcomes at classroom level.

However, as a person dedicated to equality of opportunity and outcome, a long-term and committed educationalist, I can only reserve the duty to teach what I am required to, to those I am required to teach, by any means at my disposal, responding, where I am able, to their expressed, evidenced and considered learning needs, while being prepared to respond to colleague enquiry and share my practice. However, one perhaps should try to avoid undermining the role of the learner. A former youth worker now an Associate Lecturer with the Open University reminded me;

*The teacher's job is to teach, the learner's job is to learn, but this equation is far more complex than its deceptive simplicity in presentation suggests. Firstly, I think the potential inter-changeability of roles proposed by Freire (amongst others) points to one potential level of complexity; however I also think some jump on this too quickly and use it to admonish those who dare to teach, quickly demanding their right to occupy the teacher role without considering what they are brining to it. 'The slave begins by demanding justice and ends by wanting to wear the crown'. (Camus, A:1951).*

*The Teacher/Learner role, rather than the teacher/learner dichotomy does however offer some points of potential departure from the banal experience many tolerate. I can provide witnesses, in higher education. However, I think the focus within many debates over emphasises the role of the teacher.*

*As a learner I pursued avenues and paths that were laid down by my teachers, however I was also pursuing and creating a narrative of which I was the main author, in some instances my teachers became co-authors, others were wannabe editors, or sub-editors. The point I'm trying to make here is that many explorations of teaching lack the authentic voice of the learner.*

*I remember talking with one of my teachers about their work at Masters level. This person was looking at the experiences of two supervisees in supervision from their perspective. I remember this teacher recounting that that the supervisee, who had what was judged the 'weaker supervisor', recounted the greater learning. I am not trying to make too much here in terms of a causal relationship, however I do think it offers some insight into the folly of overly trying to regulate or engineer the learning environment. I think we have an example here of a learner's ability to differentiate the difference in terms of teacher ability, experience and potential for learning. The potential to swing the other way and blame the inadequate supervisor and subsequent experience for a lack of learning is great here, so the learner becomes a critical component in the equation.*

> *Tell me, and I will listen.*
> *Show me, and I will understand.*
> *Involve me, and I will learn.*
> Lakota Proverb

The writer, author and broadcaster Jonathan Meades, echoing the likes of Socrates, recently called scepticism, cynicism and doubt the *highest human qualities*[9]. For Meades, resonant of amongst others Al-Ghazali and Descartes, the more certain we are of the truth of something, the more we should question it. This is to some extent moderated by Denis Lindley, an influential British statistician, who argued (2006),

*There are some things that you know to be true, and others that you know to be false; yet, despite this extensive knowledge that you have, there remain many things whose truth or falsity is not known to you. We say that*

*you are uncertain about them. You are uncertain, to varying degrees, about everything in the future; much of the past is hidden from you; and there is a lot of the present about which you do not have full information. Uncertainty is everywhere and you cannot escape from it.*

A colleague involved in the training of education of youth workers reflected

*I do like the emphasis on doubt and always ensure that I keep it at the forefront of my teaching. I remember something that Rabbi Lionel Blue said in one of his broadcasts: 'Doubt is something precious that helps you grow up'.*

As such, as educationalists, perhaps we should at least consider being tolerant and involved with the questioning and/or adaptation of received methods and to that extent risk being uncertain of culturally[10] prescriptive routes and routines? This would probably mean taking on the responsibility to be part of a more expansive project of communal discovery of alternative avenues.

This said, doubt is not the opposite to trust (that would be distrust). Trust is something earned and given (or withdrawn or withheld) as well as felt, so while I trust myself to be conscientious in my practice on the strength of my qualifications, experience and reputation this does not override my possible doubts about my methodology. The same would be true of my extension of trust towards my colleagues. However, part of my trust in their professional judgement is that they will use their academic freedom that inculcates their capacity to doubt and be sceptical about theory and method. Hence I do not need to constantly scrutinise my colleague's practice to trust them to do their jobs punctiliously as I trust them to share their practice and doubts about the same with me and others as they see fit and necessary; I trust them to doubt.

Of course if I or those I work with in education continue to do the same old thing in the same old way and we become so convinced that all this is 'correct' then there is relatively little that is new to share, analyse or even talk about.

A colleague in higher professional education commented on these latter perspectives;

*The willingness to embrace such a contract does not seem to be universal. But I think the willingness to risk oneself in relation to others is key, as is the willingness to embrace uncertainty and doubt, whilst retaining sufficient hope and trust to at least survive and not be crushed. Here our heroes are; Sisyphus[11] and Youssarian![12]*

Bureaucratic or informal orthodoxy and/or obedience to set-in-stone institutional/communal pedantic creeds might be enforced by public/ institutional discipline or the ostracism of tittle-tattle to implement situations wherein all are 'singing from the same hymnal' in the same way, but in the last analysis are we not all the poorer for this? Are professional judgement and academic freedom often too easily subsumed by 'concerns for consistency' enforced by the fulcrum of academic boards menaced or manipulated by the self pronounced guardians/inquisitors of institutional faith or form, a sort of academic version of courtly manners or credo?

Those who identify the heretic become champions of homogeneity. This tortured soul pitifully scrabbles up the greasy pole of their own ambition, using the friction of compliance to precious standardisation and/or betraying a kind of contorted transference of their own self loathing, they work to brand the labelled dissenter, like Thomas Stockmann, an *Enemy of the People* (see Ibsen 1994, Miller 2010). The end game is the excommunication of the nonconformist via contractual 'book, bell and candle'. A detached youth worker told me.

*This reminds me of bell hooks - in terms of the joy in teaching and being critical and flexible. She writes of being in demand by students while being treated with suspicion or downright hostility by colleagues.*

*Alea iacta est* [13] despite perhaps achieving learner satisfaction and consistency in terms of required outcomes relative to colleague performance, evidencing the myths of institutional blasphemy to be fallacious.

> *The test of a good teacher is not how many questions she can ask her pupils that they will answer readily, but how many questions she inspires them to ask her which she finds it hard to answer* - Alice Wellington Rollins

While we might not be condemned to the Crucible of Salem wherein the accuser rules by purloining the authority of the Witch Master General and we all become versions of John Proctor, Rebecca Nurse or the Reverend Parris[14], such parables set in historic fact should not be ignored. There has been, for some time, a tide of conservatism rising in some spheres of higher professional education, perhaps out of insecurity or maybe just a reflection of the path some parts of the field are currently taking.

Institutional entities and by association those of us employed by the grace of the success of the same, are lost without observance of regulation and teachers need to follow rules and policy is indisputably a taken. But should we not, as educationalists, with a commitment to improving practice and outcomes, have the liberty to explore alternative (not necessarily altogether different) paths to get where we need to go? We need of course share and adhere to general purposes, aims and outcomes and strive for consistency in the same, anything else would be not only indicative of an over inflated academic ego, it would be a form of fraud in that we are professionals working to contracts (in the shape of job descriptions). A former youth worker now and academic and trainer argued;

*I have been toying with Bourdieu's ideas for some time and wonder if the place of the teacher within the institution and the inter-professional relationship are akin to the 'symbolic violence' in the form of 'pedagogic action'; an imposition of a 'cultural arbitrary', referred to as 'diffuse education'. Our explorations are perhaps necessarily cited in the struggle between conforming to the emerging hegemonic forces of standardisation, within which it is difficult to reclaim the term 'learning outcome' for 'the learner' from 'the institution', and an informed commitment to education as the 'practice of freedom' (after Freire, hooks etc.) on the teachers and learners part.*

> *Conform! Conform! What do you want to do – run the jury though a meat-grinder, so they all come out the same?* Drummond (Act 1; Scene II)
> Lawrence, J., Lee, R.E. (1951) *Inherit the Wind* Ballantine (p. 47)

Given its organisational definition and social purpose the role of the university in the development of educational professionals would logically seem to favour the inquisitiveness of 'what would happen if we did it like this?' over the claustrophobic 'we better not try and do it like that'. The scholarly pursuit is concerned with interpretation, debate and exploration rather than promoting discipleship and following orders. Our better selves choose principled courageousness, disciplined investigation, interest and care over timidity and back-covering caution. There are light years, in terms of energising intellect and judgement making capacities, between instructing that 'it says here…we better do that' and asking 'what might this mean…in what ways could we fulfil the task?' This said, as one youth worker reminded me, this might be idealistic;

*My comments have to be considered as someone who has been away from academic life for 8 years and someone who has spent the last few years having his enthusiasm for the work eroded by the 'corporatisation' of my practice. Apologies if I come across as even more jaded and cynical than usual.*

*It is a utopian vision of education, whether it be formal or informal, that a situation can exist wherein teachers/educators are free to inspire, to challenge and be challenged, although this is congruous with sound educational theory it is incongruous with the modern political and social climate.*

Educational Puritanism has its corollaries. To paraphrase Meades (2009)[15] perhaps colourlessness is associated with cleanliness and so godliness and that this explains the mental fast that fettishizes root over branch, causing a drive to replicate to suffocate the aspiration to initiate. However, while all incarnations of the Stasi have a price, both in terms of finance and morale, imagination costs nothing.

A youth worker who qualified more than a decade ago now told me;

*As a father of four young children (which takes up much of my time and energy when I'm not working) I have been astounded at how my offspring developed distinct personalities from a very young age. The children have all been brought up in the same household. My wife and I have very similar values and outlooks on life, yet my kids, from a very early age, have all displayed different behaviours, talents, likes, dislikes and rates of development. If ever there was tangible evidence of the need for differentiated teaching styles our family are it. And, whilst training at College, I indulged myself in the freedom to adopt any academic approach to my assignments that I wished (within reason). This ability to tailor my learning according to my interests, experience and values was one of the reasons that I found my time studying for professional qualification thoroughly rewarding and why I was able to engage with the course fairly successfully. For this experience of differentiated teaching I thank those at the College who made it possible.*

Innovation may not start with 'learning revolutions' or a 'commitment to chaotic insubordination' (although each have their charms). A youth worker recollected how a particular group of learners took some control over their education while breaking away from the norm;

*When working in a junior school about twelve years ago I was invited to their launch of the new 'computer suite'. I was expecting great things but when I arrived I was shown two computers (which had been donated) in the corridor between two class rooms. At first myself and the other guests were puzzled as to why there was so much fuss over what seemed so little, but the enthusiasm of the head and the staff sucked us in. The young people had been actively encouraged to be involved in developing ways that that computers could be used and as a result they all had their own file, could down load their home work and school time table. This might not sound much in our modern world of computers but it was a lot then for a junior school.*

Strict regimentation, uniformity, conformity and inflexibility of method are the antitheses of imaginative and innovative teaching, while being diametrically opposed to the best the university can be; *plures sentential, plures mores* – this is perhaps the fuel of curiosity which might be understood as the midwife of improvement and the positive adaptive force that education can be.

> *One looks back with appreciation to the brilliant teachers, but with gratitude to those who touched our human feelings. The curriculum is so much necessary raw material, but warmth is the vital element for the growing plant and for the soul of the child.* - Carl Jung

> *It frightens me to imagine the state of learning in this world if everyone had your driving curiousity* – Drummond, Act 1; Scene II, Lawrence, J., Lee, R.E. (1951) *Inherit the Wind* Ballantine (p. 91)
>
> *Lady, when you lose your power to laugh, you lose your power to think straight* – Drummond, Act 1; Scene II, Lawrence, J., Lee, R.E. (1951) *Inherit the Wind* Ballantine (p. 50)

## NOTES

[1] I know many (probably including myself) see this as condescending term. I include it as it is widely used in the higher professional education sector. However, if we are to have a truly inclusive educational environment perhaps what was once thought of as education's 'traditional' (conventional) clientele will itself become seen for what it probably was (prosaic and elitist)?

[2] Group domination is a situation arising out of someone being prepared to take over while others give up their authority/relinquish responsibility. However, the seemingly dominant person can be viewed as a sort of group slave, doing the work of the group while everyone else sits back. Sometimes a bonus of this type of interaction for those taking on the role of the dominated is that when things go wrong they can accuse the person they have effectively encouraged or inveigled into doing their work of being a tyrant. This turns the one time apparent potentate into a scapegoat. In this process the ostensibly strong are in fact weak while the seemingly meek dominate the discourse using the power of their seeming weakness, looking for sympathy/pity while seemingly liberating themselves from the clutches of the former dictator (dupe).

[3] Post-secondary or tertiary education

[4] According to Lee's (2008) character George Brown, *If you use it right, tradition's not something that smothers you – tradition's something that sets you free* (p. 69). One of the strong messages in Lee's work is that things are, to a large extent, what you make of them – how we exert our influence and authority on them. *Teaching is not a lost art, but the regard for it is a lost tradition.* - Jacques Barzun

[5] Anything a person thought to have 'weak psychological egoism' intentionally undertakes is done with **at least with the expectation** of achieving self-regarding ends. Strong psychological egoism is thought to be demonstrated when whatever someone does they **always intend** thereby to realize a self-regarding end. Mercer argues that to understand the motivation behind an action, we need to understand the force of the consideration that motivates an individual's activity.

[6] One experienced youth worker commented, *The introduction of the National Curriculum in the 1980s might be thought of as the achievement of a zenith of bureaucratic centralisation*

[7] In our society 'non-adults' are treated/characterised as 'immature', 'adolescent', 'underdeveloped', 'lacking experience' and so on, all euphemisms for 'not fully human'. The author does not subscribe to these types of deficit models while recognising and empathising with the 'fully human' responses (resistance) made by young people/learners to the same (labelled 'rebellion', 'apathy' etc.). The point being made here however is that these types of depreciations can become replicated in group learning situations and trigger predictable reactions given the social history of childhood and oppression/exploitation of young people.

[8]   *Universitas* was the term originally applied only to the corporation of students and masters within the *stadium* - it was always modified, as *universitas magistrorum* or *universitas scholarium*, or *universitas magistrorum et scholarium*. Toward the end of the 14th century the 'stand alone' term began to be used, the exclusively meaning a *self-regulating community of teachers and scholars* whose corporate existence had been recognized and sanctioned by civil or ecclesiastical authority - Encyclopaedia Britannica: History of Education. *The development of the universities.*

[9]   *Isle of Rust*

[10]  This alludes to academic/institutional culture

[11]  Sisyphus, a figure of Greek mythology, was condemned to repeat forever the same meaningless task of pushing a boulder up a mountain, only to see it roll down again.

[12]  Capt. John Joseph Yossarian is a fictional character and protagonist in Joseph Heller's novel *Catch-22* and its sequel *Closing Time.* Yossarian's motivation is summed up in this quote: *He had decided to live forever or die in the attempt, and his only mission each time he went up was to come down alive.*

[13]  The die has been cast

[14]  See Miller (2000)

[15]  *The Football Pools Towns*

## REFERENCES

Adorno, T. W., et al. (1994). *The authoritarian personality (Studies in prejudice).* W Norton & Co.

Barrow, R., & Woods, R. (1988). *An introduction to philosophy of education.* Routledge.

Clough, P., & Nutbrown, C. (2002). *A student's guide to methodology: Justifying enquiry.* Sage.

Compayre, G. (2009). *Pestalozzi and elementary education.* BiblioBazaar.

Decourcy, D., Fairchild, L., & Follet, R. (2007). *Teaching Romeo and Juliet: A differentiated approach.* Natl Council of Teachers.

Dodge, J. (2006). *Differentiation in action: A complete resource with research-supported strategies to help you plan and organize differentiated instruction.* Teaching Strategies.

Ekwunife, J. A. (1987). *Technology and secondary school science education: How can non-formal education help?* Cardiff: University College.

Fairclough, N. (2001). *Language and power.* Longman.

Freire, P. (1998). *Pedagogy of freedom: Ethics, democracy and civic courage* (P. Clarke, Trans.). Lanham, MD: Rowman and Littlefield.

Fröbel, F. (2009). *The education of man.* BiblioBazaar.

Green, L. (2008). *Music, informal learning and the school.* Ashgate.

Hall, L. (2008). *The pitmen painters.* Faber and Faber.

Meades, J. (2009). *Off Kilter* Episode 2 'Isle of Rust' and Episode 3 'The Football Pools Towns' - Campbell, A. (Producer) BBC Four.

Mercer, M. (2001, September). In Defence of weak psychological egoism in *Erkenntnis* (Vol. 55, Number 2, pp. 217–237). Springer Netherlands.

Merttens, R., Boole, M., & Grady, K. (Illustrator) (2000). *Chat Maths.* BASS Publications.

Ibsen, H. (1997). *An enemy of the people.* Faber and Faber.

Lindley, D. V. (2006). *Understanding uncertainty.* Wiley Blackwell.

Miller, A. (2000). *The crucible: A play in four acts.* Penguin Classics.

Miller, A. (2010). *An enemy of the people.* Penguin Books.

Peters, R. S. (1966). *Ethics and education.* George Allen Unwin.

Tomlinson, C. A., Brimijoin, K., & Narvaez, L. (2008). *The differentiated school: Making revolutionary changes in teaching and learning.* ASCD.

Walsh, P. (1993). *Education and meaning.* Cassell.

Wilby, P. (2009, September 22, Tuesday). Intellectual guru seeks 'system redesign' of secondary education. *The Guardian.*

*Simon Frost* is Senior Lecturer in Informal Education,(Youth Work, Community Learning and Development) at the YMCA George Williams College, London. Since qualifying as a professional youth and community worker in 2001, he has continued to develop materials for the ethics and values module for level 3 students. Through the completion of a Masters Degree in Values in Education, (Philosphical Perspectives) and his work with undergraduate youth and community work students he continues to grapple with the question: how is it that we ought to behave? This is a question that has far reaching implications philosophically on many levels which most recently led to his involvement in a new Advanced Professional Certificate in Youth Work and Human Rights.

# CAN YOUTH WORKERS WORK *WITH* YOUNG PEOPLE? PHILOSOPHICAL PERSPECTIVE IN YOUTH WORK

## INTRODUCTION

Since the inception of youth work towards the end of the 18$^{th}$ century in the form of the early settlements and the newly founded YMCA movement through to the current contexts of youth work practice there has been a strong sense that youth workers work *with* young people. The idea of working *with* implies a number of principles that inform youth work practice. These include, amongst others, voluntary participation, responding to the needs of young people, and encouraging the potential of young people. In contrast the idea of working *on* forms part of a critical discourse amongst many of the same youth workers concerned that current youth work practice is restricting choice, expecting young people to conform, and utilizing youth work as a means of ensuring young people engage effectively in employment, education and training. *Prima facie* this appears to be a relatively straight forward argument – from an ethical point of view if we value freedom, choice and voluntary relationships, youth workers should work *with* young people. However, behind this either or view of youth work exists a number of distinctions and contra perspectives that provide a more complex picture. In separating out the practice of working *with* and working *on* one risks making the normative assumption that youth workers ought to work *with* young people rather than working *on* young people. In contrast there are a number of arguments that show youth workers do not work *with* young and neither can they work *with* young people.

What follows then is an attempt to unpack the idea of working *with* young people, firstly by looking at how the idea of working *with* is constructed. Having established criteria for working *with* young people sections 2 and 3 will begin to examine a number of contra perspectives drawing on ideas from political philosophy, learning theory, counseling and educational aims thus creating a tension between working *with* and working *on* young people. Primarily then the first three sections are a group of abstract ideas occasionally augmented with examples from practice. In contrast section 4 begins to explore working *with* and *on* young people in the context of practice. It is at this stage that the complex interplay between working *with* and working *on* starts to take shape. Once we are able to see this interplay in context it becomes possible to consider a number of ethical perspective that support the idea that youth workers should work *on* young people.

# SECTION 1

WORKING *WITH* YOUNG PEOPLE

The starting point then is the idea of working *with* young people. What is it that is being inferred in the statement youth workers work with young people? On a literal level it seems obvious that youth workers work with young people otherwise youth workers would not be youth workers. By definition youth workers need young people to work *with* to fulfill their role. However for the purposes of this essay, the term *with* is taken to mean more than work that involves young people. Implicit within the term are a number of normative claims, namely the importance of voluntary relationship as a means to fostering learning, equality and mutuality, (Smith and Smith 2006:16, Spence 2007:4). This approach is more concerned with the process rather than the outcome. Success comes from those who are interested in and motivated to work *with* young people, responding to their interests and their input (Hirsch, 2002:9). Central to the idea of working *with* young people are three important distinctions which need to be considered in establishing the idea of working *with*. The first of these is concerned with the subject of intervention and whether non intervention implies working *with* and intervention implies working *on*. The second distinction is concerned with the relationship between the young person and the youth worker. Is the relationship between the youth worker and the young person voluntary or are youth workers able to coerce young people to behave in ways that they might not choose or desire. The third distinction considers whether work with young people is based on a deficit model or can a potential model be applied.

***Intervention verses non intervention*:** The distinction of intervention verses non intervention is not a straight forward separation.

Firstly one needs to consider who is doing the intervening, for example, is it just the state or do the voluntary sector and other non statutory bodies also intervene? If it can be shown that certain youth work agencies work *with* young people whilst other youth work agencies work *on* young people then there are grounds to consider whether those who are working *with* young people take ethical precedent as an approach over those working *on* young people.

Behind this discussion is a tension in the field of youth work which questions the legitimacy of state intervention by asking the question should youth work be thought of as something that is distinct from state control (Davies 2005b). Arguably the state has a duty to intervene in the lives of young people; the question is should the state utilize youth work to intervene in the lives of young people? The legitimacy of state intervention is a key concept in political philosophy, but what we are faced with here is a concern that the state has taken control of something (youth work) that historically existed outside the state. Youth work has undergone a process of change and now the state uses youth work for its own purposes. It is fair to say that the state favours an overt interventionist approach that is informed by the preconceived needs of young people in relation to political, social and economic need.

> *The Government expects local authorities, in partnership with voluntary bodies and others, for example not for profit and private sector organizations, to demonstrate strategic leadership and to have a clear understanding of the local circumstances which impact upon the lives of young people. Local authorities will, with the co-operation of their partners, carefully identify, assess and analyze the nature of the needs of young people throughout their area.*
> DfES 2002:11

An example of this youth work model would be something like the government initiative Positive Activities for Young People (PAYP) (DFES 2006), which works to divert young people who are at risk of social exclusion using positive activities. Young people are identified and targeted by a range of professionals including the youth service, youth offending teams and local authorities. Young people are then encouraged to take part in PAYP, (ibid). Participation is monitored and young people are able to gain accreditation for the activities they engage in.

With what has been described here one has to be careful not to equate the state as being interventionist and the non statutory/voluntary sector as being non interventionist. In contrast the voluntary relational responsive approach of youth work is still a form of intervention inasmuch it is concerned with young people's values and the sort of people they are likely to become in adult life (Young 1999). Even youth work based on an Informal Education model (Mahoney (2004:28) is a form of intervention. By putting themselves in a situation where the youth worker is trying to ensure that the process of youth work invites the young person to share their own interests – the youth worker is in effect intervening. We see too from history the early settlement movement, pioneers of youth work, intervening:

> *If men and women from universities lived for some time among the poor in London and in other cities, they could 'do a little to remove the inequalities of life'*
> Barnett 1884:272

Another example would be Christian youth work, which in itself includes a dimension of missionary activity/intervention which is driven by the view that young people need to undergo faith conversions and develop spiritually (Buckeridge 2005).

With this in mind if one were to say that the interventionist approach denotes working *on*, one would also have to say that all youth work is working *on*, on the premise that all youth work, regardless of sector is based on some form of intervention.

The second separation that informs the distinction of intervention verses non intervention is the idea of predetermined intervention and non-predetermined intervention. By predetermined one is referring to a situation where the needs of the young people have already been decided in contrast to a non predetermined approach where the youth worker is free to respond to the interests of the young person, in this sense trying to determine with the young person what they need; previously described as Informal Education (Mahoney, 2004:28).

On the premise that all youth work is intervention based, not all interventions are necessarily predetermined by an existing agenda. [At this stage in the discussion the distinction is not about whether or not one ought to intervene in the lives of the young people, rather how youth workers intervene in the lives of young people.]

Logically the more the youth worker has to follow predetermined interventions, the less flexibility there is for the young person's interest to come out in the relationship they have with the youth worker, whereas in the interventions of a youth worker not bound by a predetermined curriculum with set targets, the youth worker is free to focus on the process of youth work rather than a specific end product (Mahoney 2004:26). Here there is more scope for the youth worker to respond to the agenda of the young person, engaging the young person, fostering and encouraging the ideas of the young person rather than working towards predetermined targets. With this in mind one might say that the less predetermined the intervention the more scope there is to work *with*, and vice versa.

***Voluntary verses coercive relationship:*** The second distinction can be found in the nature of the relationship between the young person and the youth worker - those who work *with* young people and voluntary relation-ships as opposed to those who work *on* young people, where the young people are being coerced into acts they neither desire or choose.

Initially then one might say that if the young person is free to separate themselves from the youth worker at any time without further consequence then the relationship between the youth worker and the young person is voluntary. One could even argue that this type of relationship applies to all youth work sectors. For example statutory youth work, which is clearly driven by targets, is still dependant on the voluntary nature of the relationship between the young person and the youth worker. In almost all cases young people are free to attend or not attend youth work provision except in exceptional cases where attendance may be required as part of a court order. The young person has a choice over whether or not to engage and participate. However, has the young person acted independently in choosing to engage or has the youth worker acted in such a way that the young person has no choice but to engage, what we might call coercion (Aquinas 1920)? This is not a straight forward question and an example might help. Imagine a young person has a particular desire, for example to swear at other people and they go ahead and swear at young people. Here we could say they have acted freely. The desires and the actions of the young person are said to be voluntary – one could even argue that the young person has acted independently (Pink, 2003:27). However if the situation where to change and the youth worker from their position of authority were to intervene and managed to persuade the young person to stop swearing– has the young person acted voluntarily by choosing not to swear or has the young person been coerced into not swearing? For a young person not to be coerced there would need to be genuine choice without consequences; they would need to know that there is an alternative choice. In this instance a young person who is able to exercise control over their own actions may in turn be subject to internal pressure to conform in that with choice we see responsibility. A young person who wittingly makes a choice is then compelled to take responsibility for their actions. (Dworkin, 1988:68) This is to the advantage of the youth worker who wants to coerce a young person in that they are in a position to create situations were the young person is under pressure to make certain informed choices. Whilst the young person has a choice in whether or not they engage with the youth worker, the youth worker is still in a position to put pressure on the young person to behave in a certain way. This is dependent on two things, firstly the willingness to accept, or the lack of agency to resist the authority of the youth worker and secondly the young person being prepared to take responsibility for their actions. With this in mind there will be some situations when a youth worker might be able to regulate the choices a young person is able to make, creating situations were the young person will feel pressured to conform. This can be achieved by making value judgments that put pressure on the young person they are working *with/on*, for example, you need to do x, otherwise you cannot achieve y and y should be desirable to you; moreover if you do not achieve y it is your fault because of the choice you made.

So far then the idea that the relationship between the youth worker and the young person is voluntary is not merely dependent on whether the young person chooses to engage with the youth worker. Once accepted by the young person, the youth worker is essentially in a position of authority which derives from those who are in a position to confer authority on youth workers, i.e. the state, the church, the voluntary sector and so on. Arguably the young person has made a voluntary choice to accept the authority of the youth worker, but at what cost? Once the young person has chosen to engage, the youth worker is then in a position to influence the choices the young person makes. From a Foucaultian perspective those in power or conduits of power i.e. youth workers, are in a position to use knowledge as a way of subjugating young people - that is *'being made subject to, being governed by institutionalized forces that control and frame.'* (Foucault 1982:213). From the same perspective youth workers would be seen as acting as agents of normalization combining hierarchical observation with normative judgment, what Foucault describes as power/knowledge (Gutting 2003). Through observing young people and engaging young people in thinking about the norms of acceptable behaviour in relation to their own behaviour- youth workers are essentially perpetuating a particular discourse that is used to govern the way in which the youth worker regards the young person. Whilst the youth worker is not always capable of coercing the young person to act in a particular way, it can still be argued that the youth worker is part of a broader disciplinary strategy of social reform. If the young person accepts this message then youth workers are free to continue to work from a position of authority. It is also worth noting that the Foucaultian perspective of youth work applies to both predetermined and non predetermined/ responsive interventions. There is just as much scope for a youth worker to persuade young people by telling them what to think in response to the interests of the young person. For example a youth worker responding to concerns a young person has about attending school might just as conceivably reiterate political discourse on the importance of being in education. The issue here is to what extent does the youth worker uses discourse to direct the decisions of the young person? The more a young person accepts the authority of the youth worker and the more the youth worker works from a position of authority - the more the youth worker can be seen to be working *on* young people.

Central to this discussion then is the importance of choice and the way in which the youth worker is able to put pressure on young people to make certain choices. To remove any aspect of compulsion the youth worker would have to emphasize the importance of autonomy, encouraging the young person to think for themselves, to act on their own thoughts and feelings, to rationalize, to question and to challenge. The youth worker would also need to recognize the importance of encouraging the young person to have a sense of ownership about what they want to do (McNair 1996:233). A useful model here is Habermas' ideal speech situation (Pusey, 1987:73), where the dynamics of the relationship change so that any claim can be defended or questioned, where there are no constraints made by the role of those engaging in the dialogue and where there is commitment towards discovering truth.

> *If we (youth workers) accept Habermas's 'ethics of discourse' we are more likely to exhibit a commitment to listening without interrupting, concentrating on one issue before moving on to another and managing our competitive instincts.*
> Tiffany 2003:103

**Deficit model of working with young people verses potentiality model of working with young people:** In this third and final distinction one is concerned with the separation of those who view youth work as being based on a deficit model and those who view youth work as being based on a potentiality model. In contrast to a deficit model of young people, Spence (2006:2) suggests that youth work ought to be:

> *Underpinned by a commitment to working with an open potentiality model beginning with the present experiences of young people responding to their present needs and building on this to situate their learning in a wider social context. This contrasts with the problem based interventions with individuals which derive from a deficit model of young people that defines them as a 'risky' time of 'becoming' rather than as a time of being.*
> Spence 2006:2

In the potentiality model the identification of need is dependant on the voluntary participation of the young person, it is only with the young person that need can be identified.

> *Relationships are important because it is in the context of being with and sharing with others that people are supported to create and recreate themselves, take charge of their relationships (with self and others), actively engage in their community and contribute to the world.*
> Young, 1999:63

Inherent in the potentiality model is the normative assumption that it is important that young people discover themselves for themselves rather than conforming to someone else's dictate.

In contrast the deficit model predetermines need and young people are objectified.

Indicative of such an approach are current statutory directives for youth services that are meant to ensure that youth work is based on a curriculum which is able to demonstrate the following:

- **content:** *a set of learning outcomes derived from themes or topics and based on needs;*
- **pedagogy:** *ways of teaching and learning so that these outcomes can be achieved; and*
- **assessment**: *performance criteria so that judgments can be made about whether or not these learning outcomes have been achieved; and an outline of processes by which these criteria can be applied.*

DfES 2002:27

The deficit model of working *on* young people is not exclusive to the statutory sector, for example, Christian youth work, as previously mentioned, will often refer to the salvation of young people as one of its goals – in other words what is missing from the lives of young people is God:

*Our hope is that the young people may recognise and respond to the Christian faith, which is the basis of our work, and which we believe gives true meaning and direction for life.*
www.salmonyouthcentre.co.uk (2008)

In practice this means that many youth workers are engaging in activities that are designed to improve young people.

Common to both the concept of deficit and potentiality models of youth work is the idea of need. In contrast, the distinction between deficit and potentiality models is perhaps best understood in terms of how the need is identified. In the deficit model need is often based on a predetermined curriculum and values, certain areas provide the focus for the relationship. The youth worker is bound by a curriculum or certain values which in turn can restrict the youth worker from being able to work with the young person's agenda; moreover the youth worker has the added pressure of meeting targets which will inevitably inform the direction in which the youth worker wants to take the relationship with the young person. In contrast the potentiality model is open to the contribution of the young person to determine their own needs.

[A contra perspective would be that it is morally acceptable to see young people in deficit in that young people are not in a position to be aware of everything they need to get on in life. Certain knowledge is both required and inevitable, what Pring (1995) calls the passing down of expert knowledge.]

[Another area of concern that runs through this discussion is the way in which youth work treats young people as objects rather than subjects (Barrow 1988:112). ]

## SUMMARY

At this stage one can start to see how the idea of working *with* young people is differentiated from the idea of working *on* young people. In turn a set of criteria for working *with* young people starts to emerge.

- All youth work regardless of sector is interventionist however the less predetermined the intervention, the greater the scope to work *with* young people.
- All youth work regardless of sector is based on need but approaches to determining need vary. For some need is predetermined, for others need is something that arises through conversation and listening. Where need is less predetermined there is greater to scope to work *with* young people.
- In nearly all cases the relationship between the youth worker and the young person is negotiated, however this needn't mean that the relationship is voluntary. Coercion and influence can also be seen to affect whether the youth worker is working *with* or *on* the young person.
- Youth work can be based on a deficit model or on a potentiality model. Seeing a young person in deficit prohibits the youth worker from working *with* the young person.
- Intervention needs to be responsive rather than predetermined.
- As far as possible there needs to be a joint commitment on the part of the young person and the youth worker to work together to identify need and potential.
- Certain values need to prevail, namely freedom of choice, autonomy, self determination and respect.
- The youth worker needs to be able to recognize when they are starting to coerce the young person into making decisions.

# SECTION 2

WORKING *WITH* YOUNG PEOPLE – A CONTRA PERSPECTIVE

In attempting to understand the overall question one has been asked to consider those grounds on which we might say that youth workers can work *with* young people. Clearly there is an argument that yes youth workers can work *with* young people as seen in the previous section. However there is also a contra perspective that youth workers cannot work *with* young people. As a starting point for this discussion we return again to the idea of intervention as something that ought to be responsive rather than predetermined if youth workers are to work *with* young people. The contra view would be that regardless of whether the intervention is responsive or predetermined, young people who are capable of expressing themselves independently are effectively undermined by those who have already intellectualized their needs. From a Foucaultian perspective this is achieved by utilizing knowledge as power (Smart, 1985:71ff). Whilst the youth worker might not wish to predetermine the needs of the young person, the youth worker is still informed by an academic understanding of young people.

The second issue is one of inclusiveness. If a youth worker has the power to include it follows that youth worker has the power to exclude. In practice there can be many areas where a youth worker is able to include young people, i.e. decision making, design, debate and so on. Yet at the same time many youth workers are operating on a level of consciousness that doesn't include young people; thinking about the situations they find themselves in as they happen, looking for new knowledge that will help them find solutions to problems they are facing within their role as youth workers, what is known by many as reflection in action (Schön 1983).

> *The practitioner allows himself [sic] to experience surprise, puzzlement, or confusion in a situation which he finds uncertain or unique. He[sic] reflects on the phenomenon before him [sic], and on the prior understandings which have been implicit in his [sic] behavior. He carries out an experiment which serves to generate both a new understanding of the phenomenon and a change in the situation.*
> (Schön 1983: 68)

The important question here is whether the young person is aware that the youth worker is reflecting in action or does the act of reflecting in action infer an internalized thought process that doesn't include the young person,

From the contra perspective being discussed here, the more reflection is exercised as an internal process, the more the worker is able to control the direction of the work with the young person. In addition to the idea of reflection in action is the idea of reflection on action where the youth worker reflects after the event has taken place, revisiting their experiences from a more objective viewpoint normally without those young people who were involved at the time. Again this allows the youth worker to operate from a level of consciousness that is unknown to the young person.

The third area of concern are the normative assumptions that underpin the intervention of the youth worker, namely the way in which discourse is used to legislate for the way in which young people participate in society. From a contra perspective it is in this context that the youth worker sees the young person in deficit. From a historical perspective we know this to be the case from the early settlement movement, when youth work was seen as a predominantly philanthropic pursuit. There was great concern amongst the upper classes that young people from the working classes needed to be moralized; such thinking was largely based on Christian teaching (Davies 1999:12), underpinned by a sense of benevolence towards the child in what has been described as:

> *the unashamed targeting of young people of working class background*
> *who were considered by many during this time of imperialism deemed*
> *not fit to contribute to the defense of the country or indeed its economy*
> (ibid).

Inherent in this form of intervention is the change that is sought after. The purpose of the youth worker is to bring about some sort of change or learning, whether that is the self realization of the young person or the intent to make men (sic) ethical (Gordon and White 1979: 51ff). Even if the youth worker's only aim is seeing the young person developing into someone who is capable of acting autonomously and exercising choice, the contra perspective would still argue that they have to work *on* the young person to get them to that stage. The youth worker is trying to make something happen to the young person – working *on* their needs by 'helping'. From a Foucaultian perspective one would need to ask whether it was necessary in the first place to intervene. In defending oneself against the contra perspective that is unfolding here, a youth worker might claim that they can work *with* the young person if they themselves have no aims. One reason for saying that the youth worker has no aims might be to show that the youth worker is open to whatever the young person brings. The youth worker does not want to be accused of influencing or coercing the young person, thus they claim to be working *with* whatever the young person brings. From a contra view point it would be hard to see how the youth worker could avoid getting into a situation where they wouldn't want the young person to think about things in a certain way; moreover because of their role as educators they are compelled to confront the young person based on the prevailing norms of society (Peters, 1981:34). In this respect the idea of having no aims can be seen as another means to be able to work *on* young people. I will come back to this idea in Section 4 when I will be using different approaches of youth work to contextualize the issues of working *with* and working *on* young people.

## SUMMARY

As with the first section a number of claims emerge that are pertinent to the argument being put forward.

– From a contra perspective, intervention suggests that young people have needs which require support; moreover young people will face difficulties if intervention is not forthcoming.
– Essentially all youth work is based on a deficit model to some extent.
– The process of reflection in action places the youth worker in an elevated position in that they are observing and analyzing their interventions separate from the young person they are working with.
– All youth work has an agenda.

All we can do for the time being is to allow the two sets of claims to sit side by side. Essentially all that has been shown thus far is that the idea of working *with* young people is largely contestable given the different view points that exist. We will return to the claims made in these last two sections in section 4 in the context of practice.

# SECTION 3

ALTERNATIVE PERSPECTIVES

The next stage in our enquiry is to compare and contrast those different ways in which people claim to work *with* and *on* others in comparative contexts. These comparisons are not chosen arbitrarily. As you will see from the discussions that follow the comparisons derive from existing connections with the field of youth work.

WORKING *WITH*, A DIALECTICAL APPROACH

To start with then one has to identify those relationships where people are claiming to be working with. Within the field of philosophy the idea of the dialectical relationship has given rise to the idea of two people working with each other whereby one starts with a particular body of knowledge (thesis) added to this body of knowledge is another view point (antithesis) resulting in something new being created (synthesis) (Collinson and Plant, 1987:149).

Imagine then two colleagues who are working together on a piece of research; two minds working together trying to work through an idea or to develop a particular theoretical perspective, dialectically they are concerned with both analysis and synthesis (Gadotti, 1996:11). There might well be some posturing as each party seeks to exert their own perspective, however there is also a sense of togetherness that is fuelled by a common aim and a shared task, with both parties remaining equal. In this scenario both parties recognize that they are working together. Crucial to the idea of working with one another is that both parties are coming from a position of knowledge, the relationship is overt and explicit in that both parties are aware of their own viewpoint. This is not the same as Illich's concern that we oughtn't to tell each other what they should learn (Illich, 1971:5). Neither party is being deliberately manipulated, there is nothing that cannot be questioned; it is even conceivable that either party might be willing to change their opinion at any given time.

Another important factor in this example is the way in which need plays its part. For the dialectic to work the contra view point is required, so is a willingness to allow oneself to be questioned, essentially using Socrates' method of systematic and methodical doubt (Gadotti, 1996:9). In this respect there is evidence of *need* in this relationship, both parties need the other to foster questioning; however this concept of need is distinct from the deficit model in that neither party is trying to 'fix' the other. In the dialectical mode the pursuit is truth, that is the only agenda. It is not something that is used to control in terms of those involved in the questioning and the thinking. In some ways what has been described here is indicative of Habermas' ideal speech situation, as previously mentioned. Hitherto then we have considered albeit a somewhat hypothetical example of working *with* another or working *together*. On the premise that one accepts this idea of working *with* the next stage is to consider this idea of working *with* in comparison to the idea of working *with* young people. Here one is being asked to consider the idea of the youth worker as a dialectician, simply committed to a dialectical approach of understanding in pursuit of truth. The role of the youth worker would simply be to engage the young person on what they know and then question based on what the youth worker already knows. In questioning the young people over what they know, the youth worker would need to encourage the young person to reciprocate with their own questions, not simply to clarify their own understanding but rather to allow the ideas of the youth worker to be challenged . For the youth worker to be able to show that they are working with a young person based on the model of the two colleagues, a number of criteria would have to be met. However when these criteria are juxtaposed with youth work practice a number of contrasts emerge:

– Both the youth worker and the young person are clear on what they know

*The youth worker because of their knowledge, born out of study and reflection in and on action, will already have a sense of where the young person needs to get to. Arguably adolescence is a period of development in which young people grow, not only physically but also mentally in terms of cognitive development. As such young people go through a process whereby their ability to understand moves from a mechanical understanding to a reasoned understanding, (Barrow & Woods, 1982:56), another way of describing this is the change from knowing to understanding. To be able to enter into the dialectical process, the young person would need to have a reasoned understanding. Given the variation amongst young people in terms of reasoned understanding it is reasonable to say that a significant number would not be clear on what they know.*

– The young person is aware that they are working with the youth worker.

*Arguably not all young people have the capacity to wittingly engage with a youth worker. If the young person does not have the wherewithal to challenge the normative values of the youth worker then there is an imbalance. Such imbalance is indicative of Friere's concern with 'banking*

*education', where essentially the person being educated remains passive to the intervention of the educator who is seen to deposit knowledge that is received uncritically (Freire. 1970:57ff).*

- The objective of the relationship is not to change the behavior of the young person, rather to discover together.

*The intervention of the youth worker is needs based, whether that be responsive or predetermined intervention. The youth worker who reacts to the needs/ interests of the young person is not working with the young person in the sense that one might work with a colleague because the intervention is a response to the need of another.*

- The focus of the task is shared and both the youth worker and the young person are susceptible to change and influence.

*To work with there is a requirement that both parties have something to contribute, two sets of knowledge. Then there is something to build upon together, with each idea moving on to the next idea and then on to the next idea until all ideas are exhausted and one remaining idea rules the remaining ideas (Strauss & Cropsey, 1963:43) In the case of the youth worker with no specific aims, this dialectical approach is not feasible. Dialectics is replaced with dialogue, with the youth worker responding to the interests of the young person, encouraging the young person to reason their experiences and ideas within a particular moral framework. Thus as Belton (2007), has argued there is no potential for creativity, the youth worker is bound by a particular set of values and beliefs that prevent the youth worker from responding as a human being.*

Essentially it is the role of the youth worker as an interventionist that prevents the youth worker from working together with a young person in a dialectical way. Boundaries, professional frames of reference, targets and the inculcation of moral norms as well as expertise and knowledge mean that the playing field between youth worker and young person is not a level one, not in the sense that two colleagues might work together *with* each other.

## WORKING *WITH*, A COUNSELING APPROACH

In response to the claim that youth workers are working *with* because they are working with the experiences of young people, it is worth considering the comparative model of person centered counseling, where in order to work *on* the client, the therapist has to first understand the client.

Historically there has been a relationship between therapeutic models of working *with* people and youth work since the 1960's when key figures in the field of youth work such as Tash (1967:148), spent a great deal of time emphasizing the importance of building quality relationship so as to be able to help young people, deemed unattached at the time, so as to develop young people socially. Whilst the current emphasis in state funded youth work is geared towards targeted outcomes, the importance of the relationship as a vehicle for helping young people remains a central theme in contemporary youth work. It is on the importance of the relationship that youth work and the field of counseling come together. For Tash et al (ibid) the relationship was the vehicle to be able to reach the young person. Here there is a similarity with the Rogerian model of counseling (Rogers, 1967:304) which identifies the need for the therapist to enter into a person to person relationship so as to be able to help. In addition, the importance of ongoing support and acceptance form tenets of both the relational youth work that Tash describes and Rogerian thinking on acceptance and trust as a premise for being able to facilitate the learning of the client.

Another important connection to be made between youth work and counseling is the way in which both the therapist and the youth worker work with the story of the client/young person. The therapist needs to be able to make sense of the client's needs if they are to be able to help. In this sense the therapist is working with what the client brings, however what the client brings is only one part of the equation. From here the therapist will, depending on their particular orientation, follow a particular set of procedures to help the client make sense of themselves and move on to a better place in their lives. Here there is a connection to be made between the experience of the client and the support that the youth worker provides to enable the young person to work out the answer to their questions; moreover it is acknowledged that the young person needs the youth worker because the youth worker is able to see the potential whereas the young person is only able to relate to the present. The view being taken here is that some young people do not have the social skills to be able to recognize and respond to the opportunities that are available to them, rather they require help to see something of their potential future (Tash, 1967:141) In the context of the contra perspective of working *with*, it is those skills and procedures that denote working *on,* trying to fix their problems. It can be argued that the client and the therapist are working together, because without the work of the client, the therapist has nothing to facilitate in terms of the clients learning (Rogers cited in Barrett Lennard, 1998:184). The contra view would be that the client is not working *with* the therapist rather they are allowing the therapist to help reconstruct the way in which they think. The client in approaching a therapist for help would do so because they see themselves as being in deficit in some way.

The comparisons between youth work and counseling/therapy are many.
– There is an agreed view that the client or the young person is in need.

- The therapist/youth worker will intervene in a responsive manner, but at the same time have an ability to look further forward than the client/ young person is initially able to recognize potential.
- In both approaches the worker/therapist is there to help the young person/client find the answers themselves.
- The position of youth worker/therapist confers an elevated status above the young person/client.
- Whilst both the therapist and the youth worker might have faith in the potentiality of the client/young person they are still in deficit inasmuch as they require the intervention of a therapist/youth worker so as to start a process of help.
- When potential is achieved, when the client/young person is able to take on a critical perspective of their own situation, so it is more likely that the client/young person becomes free to help themselves free from any compulsion or feeling of deficit (Habermas cited in Pusey, 1987:73).

BEING WITH RATHER THAN WORKING WITH

In contrast to the idea of working with is the idea of being with. Attempts have been made within the field of youth work to articulate the importance of the worker as someone who is able to help young people based on the idea of 'being with' (Fromm 1979).

> *While the having persons rely on what they have, the being persons rely on the fact that they are, that they are alive and that something new will be born if only they have the courage to let go and respond. They become fully alive in the conversation because they do not stifle themselves by anxious concern with what they have. Their own aliveness is infectious and often helps the other person to transcend his or her egocentricity. Thus the conversation ceases to be an exchange of commodities (information, knowledge, status) and becomes a dialogue in which it does not matter any more who is right.*
> Fromm 1979:42

If the worker is to be able to 'be' with the young person in the Frommian sense of the term they will need to be alive to the idea that they themselves might change or indeed learn something new about themselves, the path of learning in the Frommian sense is much more of a collaborative approach which should be informed by a lack of status, *'it flows from the 'aliveness' of the worker and their capacity to be themselves and part of conversations and encounters.'* (Smith and Smith, 2007:xii). In trying to assimilate the idea of being with young people and the role of the youth worker Smith and Smith (ibid), have not fully considered the role and purpose of the youth worker. It is conceivable that as people we can be with each other, open and alive to new ideas, willing to be challenged and so forth, as say the two colleagues working with each other; however by virtue of their appointment the youth worker has a certain status that disables their ability to be with. One way around this would be to consider what would happen if the youth worker was conceived in a different paradigm. Currently those representing youth work today fall into three areas. Firstly that part of the voluntary sector that is bound contractually to deliver state funded youth work provision, secondly public sector youth work that is regulated by the state and thirdly independent voluntary sector work with young people that is essentially free within the law to provide youth work provision without being compromised by political agendas. A good example of this sector would be faith based youth work.

However if one were to separate the youth worker from all of these contexts, essentially deprofessionalising the role of the youth worker; a youth worker would then simply be someone who chooses to 'be' with young people, not because the young person is in deficit, not as part of a develop-mental process in any formal sense, but rather as a vehicle for creativity and human flourishing. The purpose of the youth worker is only to be with the young person in a way in which other prominent adults involved in the lives of young people are not capable of because of their role in society, namely parents/carers/teachers. However such an idea requires a paradigm shift from the current conception of youth work so much so that it might not be legitimate to call such a relationship *youth work*; moreover the emergence of a relationship between a young person and an adult that is not regulated or based on some sort of natural tie i.e. a family member, is likely to be vilified.

## AUTONOMY AS AN EDUCATIONAL AIM

Hitherto this section has been concerned with looking at comparative models of working *with*. In contrast the final part of this section will briefly consider a model for working *on* young people and its relevance to the field of youth work. The starting point then is the idea that youth workers are aiming at something in their work with young people; moreover it is the aims of youth work which form the basis of any intervention. One such aim, although something of a paradox, is that young people need to be educated to be autonomous. Within the context of educational philosophy, certain criteria are required to show that the young person has indeed reached this stage. According to Frankfurts' hierarchy of desires, (Cuypers 1995), the process of reflection on first order desires is evidence of personal autonomy in that the individual is able to reflect, evaluate and choose.

*[..] autonomy is volitional harmony... autonomy is self rule; a person rules her or himself by evaluating her or his desires of the lower order according to her or his desires of the higher order. This self evaluation amounts to self government: the government of a person by the person her or himself.*
(Cuypers, 1995:131)

The aim is for the young person to be able to understand themselves in relation to the expectations of others and to possess the moral courage and critical agency to work with the arguments of others (Callan and White cited in Blake et al, 2003:97). White, J. (1990), suggests that the formation of desire and want is an important part of development in that without the desire to evaluate ones choices, one would not be in a position nor would one be disposed to evaluate, hence desire is something that needs to be fostered by teachers if young people are to be educated to be autonomous. White, (ibid) also argues that in working with children there is a need to steer them towards what is socially valuable as part of a greater objective of attaining the good life which is constituted in part by personal autonomy.

*If personal autonomy is to come out of this, it cannot run counter to all social constraints since these constraints are built in from the start... Educators need to work confidently on laying these foundations, untroubled by the thought that they are illicitly moulding children after a preconceived pattern.*
(White, 1990:77)

*Education consists essentially of the initiation of others into a public world picked out by language and concepts of a people and in encouraging others to join in exploring the realms marked out by a more differentiated forms of awareness.*
(Peters, 1966:52)

In her work on education and citizenship White, P. (1996), challenges the educational system because it creates a disparity between its aims and its practice. Whilst purporting to develop autonomous citizens, the reality is that young people are not treated autonomously. In crude terms if a young person feels oppressed by their educational experience, there is little likelihood of their wanting to contribute to society as autonomous, conscious and intellectual beings. There are obvious parallels here with the field of youth work. The question for youth workers is how might youth work promote a positive experience that will enthuse and encourage young people to want be autonomous. One way as White (ibid), suggests is to treat young people as capable of acting autonomously, encourage them to make choices, to reflect, to reason, and to work with the arguments of others. The extent to which young people are capable of and given the opportunity to act autonomously is subject to further enquiry. As seen here there is a normative assumption that being autonomous is as much an act of altruism and the benefit to society as it is about self government and making choices in that 'authentic' personal autonomy *'presupposes the impact of other people's attitudes and the larger communal concept'* (Cuypers, 1995). In essence working *on* young people to develop autonomy has a certain utilitarian quality; moreover the type of autonomy that promotes what is socially valuable (White 1990) is to be encouraged. With this in mind the idea of working *on* can be seen as something of a positive in the context of the greater good.

Slowly then our questions unfolds. We have seen how some argue that youth workers can work *with* young people and others argue that youth workers cannot work *with* young people. We have also seen that despite a number of links with comparative theory, there is not a great deal to support the idea that youth workers do work *with* young people. In contrast there are grounds to consider the importance of working *on* young people in certain contexts. At this stage no clear position has ensued regarding the normative claim that it is better to work *with* rather than to work on, although there has been a strong inference of liberal thinking on education contrasted with what might traditionally be thought of as radical perspectives in education.

# SECTION 4

## PRACTICAL PERSPECTIVES OF WORKING *WITH* AND *ON* YOUNG PEOPLE–IS IT POSSIBLE FOR YOUTH WORKERS TO WORK *WITH* YOUNG PEOPLE?

So far much of the discussion in this thesis has remained abstract, attempting to intellectualize the concept of working *with* and working *on* young people. The next stage in this research is to take the main points that have arisen in the discussion and attempt to locate them within a practice based context.

The methodology for this section is relatively straight forward. Four brief case studies reflecting a common range of youth work perspectives have been captured using auto biographical narratives. Practitioners where asked to provide a brief example from practice that centered around an event or an incident where they were working directly with a young person or a group of young people. These are then analyzed from the different perspectives identified thus far.

### SCENARIO 1 – OPEN YOUTH CLUB

A young person came into a youth club. Around that time there had been some activity in the area by one of the far right political parties. The young person came up to the youth worker and showed him a text on his mobile phone. The youth worker asked the young person who the text was from. The young person replied that the text was from someone asking them to attend a march that was taking place at the weekend. The youth worker asked the young person if they had intended to go along to the march. The young person replied yes they would be attending. The youth worker asked why this was so. The young person replied that they felt there were too many 'foreigners' in this country. The youth worker asked the young person why they felt this way and the young person replied that it had always been like this in the area. First it was the Irish then the Gypsies and Travelers and now the Blacks. The youth worker asked the young person if they knew anyone else attending the march. The young person replied that they would be attending the march with his dad and his granddad. The youth worker then took a different approach. They knew that the young person was friends with a young person who although born in the UK who had foreign parents. To fit into the area this other young person went by the name John but his real name was Yusuf. Yusuf was slightly darker in his complexion but not significantly, to all intents and purposes he wanted to and had successfully managed to form a friendship with the young person who was going to attend this march. The youth worker asked the young person about this friendship. What would he do if this political party got its way and people deemed foreigners were repatriated? The young person replied that it would be a shame but it would be best for the country and that he would write to his friend to explain his views.

This incident took place in an open youth club. There was no clear racism policy and in their role the youth worker had plenty of scope to respond to the young person rather than having to resort to overt forceful measures such as barring the young person from entering the centre. In many respects the youth worker adopted a Socratic line of enquiry. By challenging the young person over their friendship with a foreign young person, they were trying to highlight the inconsistency in their views, by showing that whilst on the one hand they were prepared to fight for enforced repatriation they were also friends with a young person who had foreign parents. In relation to the criteria for working *with* and working *on* a number of links can be made. Firstly there was a relationship between the youth worker and the young person, although it was not an equal relationship. The youth worker saw themselves in a position of authority in so far as they had already taken a view on what the young person had said and they thought that from a moral point of view it was important to work *on* what the young person was saying. They had already intellectualized the issues and come to a view. In approaching the youth worker there was a sense that the young person was allowing the youth worker to challenge their point of view by continuously asking questions. In talking to the youth worker who provided this account, we know that the youth worker was not accepting of the young person's views; rather they hoped that through logic and consistency the young person would come to the right answer. It wasn't enough to tell the young person what to think; the youth worker wanted the young person to experience the thought process that would lead to the right answer. In this respect the youth worker was trying to create a situation where the young person could see the choice that a morally autonomous person would make were they to find themselves in that particular situation. With this in mind we can see that the youth worker has an agenda. In this case it is a long term agenda to see the young people develop into a morally autonomous human being; moreover there is evidence of transparency in this process. The youth worker's value base comes across in the questions that are being asked in that the questions are designed in such a way as to show that the young person is not behaving rationally. What does not come across to the young person is the normative position of linking rational thinking and moral autonomy that is taken by the youth worker. With this in mind we can say that in terms of working *on* the young person the youth worker has no power or control over the young person, rather they are putting their faith in the process of rational thinking. The youth worker does not overtly state that the young person should accept a different point of view, rather they have a hope that the young person will come to the right conclusions by themselves. However the youth worker does see the young person as being in deficit in that they are of the view that some sort of intervention is required to change the attitude of the young person they are working with; moreover without intervention it is unlikely that the young person's conceptual framework on matters of race will be challenged.

To summarize thus far a number of new ideas emerge.

Firstly to work *on* does not necessarily mean that the youth worker has to exercise power or be coercive. By not punishing the young person for their views, the youth worker is able to use conversation to continuously engage the young person's point of view.

Secondly there may be legitimate grounds for working *on* if working *on* can be seen to contribute to the moral development of the young person.

Thirdly if the long term agenda is autonomy then there will come a point where the young person is no longer seen as being in deficit. On the premise that all youth work sees young people in deficit, any intervention that serves to shift the young person from being in deficit should be considered of value.

## SCENARIO 2 – TARGETED YOUTH WORK

The second example looks at an intervention that was predetermined. In this situation as part of a broader strategy for reducing anti social behaviour in a local area, a youth worker was asked to work with a small group of boys who had been causing disruption on an estate. Initially concerns had been raised by local residents and the anti social behaviour unit in that area had been asked to intervene. Community wardens had been deployed to the estate to find out what was happening. After talking to the boys the community wardens thought that the youth service would be able to help by diverting the young people away from the area. The youth worker was then taken on to the estate by the community wardens to meet the group who had been causing trouble. At this point the community wardens withdrew from the situation leaving the youth worker to engage with the young people. The youth worker asked the young people what they had been up to, to which the young people did not reply directly, continuing to talk amongst themselves. The youth worker then suggested that the boys had been in trouble; moreover they were known to the anti social behaviour unit and they were at risk of receiving anti social behaviour orders if they carried on getting into trouble. The youth worker then asked them if they knew about the youth centre, suggesting that it might be a good place to go and do things and it could help to keep them out of trouble. The young people appeared interested and said they would come along. When the young people first arrived they were keen to test the boundaries. They were loud and used abusive and threatening behaviour. Rather than telling the young people how to behave the youth worker asked the young people what they thought would be acceptable behaviour; however the youth worker already had a clear idea of what behaviour would be tolerated. As with the previous scenario the youth worker wants the young people to go through a thought process so that they can see why it is important to behave in a particular way, rather than simply telling the young person what was expected of them. The young people expressed some of their own ideas which the youth worker then related to the code of conduct that all members were expected to adhere to. At this point the behaviour of the group changed. They were able to recognise that if they were prepared to conform then they would be rewarded with certain activities. Arguably they started to behave because they could see they could get something out of the relationship.

After the young people had been attending the club for a number of weeks the youth worker pointed out that he thought the behaviour of the group had changed for the better. They were less confrontational both with others and amongst themselves. This comment had an adverse affect on the group. They became loud and aggressive, resulting in one member of the group being banned from the youth club. In terms of the relationship between the young people and the youth worker, the youth worker had to negotiate all the time with the group of young people. The youth worker did not have any control over their behaviour. It was only by offering an incentive that he could get the young people to calm down. However the incentive does not provide a constant hold over the young people. They realize that the youth worker wants them to comply, but they also realize that there is something in it for them; moreover they are prepared to risk losing the incentives of the youth club to show that although they have chosen to comply, they can also choose not to comply. This is evident when after being praised for the change in their behaviour they again become disruptive.

What we can say then is that the youth worker did not have any control or power over this group of young people as in the first scenario. The youth worker had no sanctions. All the youth worker was able to do was to get the young people to see that if they behaved, they could come to the youth club and therefore be less likely to get into trouble hanging around on the estate with nothing to do. In thinking about the criteria for working *on* a number of comparisons can be made. The intervention of diverting these young people away from trouble had been predetermined. Through the statutory youth service the state can be seen to intervene. There were a number of agendas being worked through, the need to reduce the group's disruptive behaviour, the need to divert the group away from trouble and the intrinsic value that is gained through engaging in activities that might be thought of as edifying to the young people in some way. In terms of diverting the behaviour of the young people into positive activities, the young people themselves had no control of the agenda.

Despite the young people not being able to influence the youth worker's agenda, the youth worker can be seen to be open about the agenda he is working to. At no point does the youth worker pretend that the intervention is anything other than it is. It could be said that such transparency shows honesty and integrity on the part of the youth worker. In this sense the youth worker wants the young people to understand the agenda he is working to. This informs the choice that the young people are making; moreover the young people can see that having made this choice they can still un-choose if they want to. Whilst the youth worker might want the young people to make certain choices, the principle of choice is more important than the choices that are made. This is important when thinking about an ethical approach to working *on* young people. Whilst youth workers are being expected to persuade and negotiate with young people to conform, the change in behaviour has to be something that the young person chooses for themselves.

Another important factor in this scenario is the issue of authority. It is only when the young people accept the youth worker's authority that he has any authority. The moment the young people choose not to accept the authority of the youth worker, so the youth worker's authority ceases. To suggest that their authority is only ever given or taken away, safeguards the young people from being manipulated and coerced into certain forms of behaviour. However this does not mean that the youth worker isn't working *on* the young person, the youth worker is still pushing a certain line, in this case it is better to conform rather than rebel; moreover the state favours those who conform and will target those who do not conform. Whilst the youth worker might not be able to directly control the behaviour of the young people, the state can and will.

## SCENARIO 3 – SCHOOLS - BASED YOUTH WORKER

In this scenario a young person comes into the inclusion centre in a school. The inclusion centre exists to work with young people who for whatever reason are at risk of or have been excluded from school. The inclusion project runs a drop in centre. The young person is extremely upset. The young person has come along out of choice. The young person hasn't made an appointment; any young person can come in to the drop in centre. It is a warm, comfortable, safe place to hang out. Young people do not need to have a reason to drop in other than perhaps to meet the youth workers or to socialize with peers. When the youth worker notices the young person enter the drop in session a number of thoughts go across her mind. Why has the young person come into the drop in, what does the young person want, what sort of mood are they in, can they expect trouble – the youth worker has worked with the young person in the past regarding her anger. The youth worker calls across the room to say hello. By the tone of the response the youth worker senses that the young person is not happy. There is another young person in the room and the worker is aware that there has been tension between these two young people in the past. The first thing the youth worker does is to try to divert the young person away from the other young person already in the room by asking if she wants to play a board game. The young person agrees. The youth worker can see from the expression on the young person's face that they are upset. Rather than ask the young person what is wrong, the youth worker attempts to distract the young person from her feelings by asking questions. The youth worker knows that the young person's favorite soap opera was on the night before. She asks the young person if she saw it and what she makes of one of the storylines for the main character. As the young person begins to talk, the youth worker looks for a way to compliment the young person. She notices the young person has done something different to her hair, then she makes a comment along the lines of 'I hope you're not going to beat me again, you're really good at this game aren't you.' After a short period the young person appears more relaxed. It is at this point that the youth worker starts to ask the young person about their day, but again not specifically asking about why she was upset. The youth worker wants the young person to take a step back and see how the whole day has been so far rather than the specific incident that had led to her coming into the drop in centre in a bad mood. By the time the young person gets to talk about why she is upset, she is much calmer than when she first came in, she has been complimented a number of times, she is feeling okay about herself and she has identified a number of good things that have happened rather than the one incident that had upset her.

In terms of working on the young person the youth worker is drawing on what she already knows about the young person's behaviour, about what makes the young person angry and what makes the young person calm. The youth worker knows that her intervention around the particular issue is more likely to be effective if the young person calms down first. The youth worker employs a range of deliberate tactics to shift the mood of the young person, such as diverting the young person's attention, trying to alter the way the young person is thinking about herself at that time and encouraging the young person to be more objective. This is achieved through the specific questions that are being asked. The youth worker is deliberately considering the need to make some sort of intervention. The youth worker, given her professional understanding of the situation, has started to intellectualize the needs of the young person. The intervention itself was both predetermined and responsive in that the youth worker's agenda as a behavioral mentor in a school was predetermined, but the intervention itself was responsive. Whether or not the young person was aware of this process is not clear. The young person may have subconsciously known that the youth worker would attempt to bring calm to the situation. Perhaps this is what the young person was hoping for. What we can say is that when the youth worker was reflecting in action (Schön, 1983), evaluating the situation, deliberately trying to create a safe, open environment for the young person, it was they who took the responsibility for identifying the opportunity, not the young person. It was the youth worker who took responsibility for working *on* the feelings of the young person. The young person allowed the youth worker to work on her feelings. The youth worker describes her interventions as trying to hold the young person, making them feel safe. Whilst the young person was happy to let the youth worker take on and work with her feelings, there was no agreement that this was what was needed. In allowing the youth worker to take on their feelings the young person was presenting herself in deficit, as someone who needed the help of another.

## SCENARIO 4 – GROUP WORK

This scenario is about piece of work that a youth worker undertook with a group of young musicians who wanted to form a band. As individuals the group were more than competent. They wanted somewhere to rehearse. The group did not ask for a youth worker to be involved. The youth club had employed a youth worker with some musical knowledge to support the young people during their rehearsal sessions. The youth worker would help to set up the equipment, stand in on a particular instrument if there was someone missing and help the group to work around conflict issues that arose. This was appreciated by the group. There were a number of distinctive features about this group. In terms of knowledge and musicianship, the young people were far more qualified than the youth worker. When it came to musical arrangement it was the youth worker who learnt from the young people. It was difficult to see what authority the youth worker had.

The young people were focused and disciplined, the young people were not disruptive. There were no targets set for the group, they could work at their own pace. If they wanted to continue they could, if they wanted to discontinue they could as well.

In one particular session the band were having a disagreement about who was going to play what instrument on a particular track. One of the newer members of the group was an extremely accomplished lead guitarist but he had been playing the bass guitar just so that he could be in the band. It was another member of the group who suggested that he should play the lead guitar. The young person playing the bass guitar became quite excited at this prospect but was also aware that he was fairly new to the group and did not want to upset the existing dynamics. At this point the youth worker intervened. The worker asked the group how they felt about taking on different roles in the group at different times. What effect would this have in terms of performing to others if they kept swapping instruments? Did they feel threatened or upset by this suggestion? Here the youth worker was attending to the groups' needs to work through a potential area of conflict. The youth worker did not offer any specific comment on the situation itself, however the youth worker was keen that the young people talk to each other about their feelings and how they themselves were going to try to find a way forward. The youth worker's intervention was designed to benefit the group. Effectively the youth worker became a group worker, trying to work *on* the group to help manage conflict and threat.

## ANALYSIS

Prior to starting this chapter there were essentially two main perspectives that had emerged. The first perspective is that it is better to work *with* young people rather than *on* young people and the second perspective is that it is not possible to work *with* young people only *on* young people.

## Perspective 1

| Working *with* | Working *on* |
|---|---|
| – Relationships | – Fixing people |
| – Fostering Leaning | – People are in deficit/ need help |
| – Equality | – Intervention based – predetermined |
| – Mutuality | – Duty to intervene |
| – Emphasis on process rather than content and outcomes | – Targeted |

| | |
|---|---|
| – Intervention based (responsive) | – Involuntary |
| – Choice | – Coercive |
| – Autonomy | – Control |
| – Potentiality | – Discourse |
| – Dialectical | |

However in light of evidence contained within the range of scenarios presented at the beginning of this chapter, there are grounds to consider that the distinction between working *with* and *on* is less clear within a practical context.

- All youth work is based on a relationship of sorts. Issues such as trust, motivation, care, role, authority do vary within different types of relationships. For example the worker in the music group and the youth worker in the school both had the trust of the young person, there was also evidence to suggest that both of these workers cared for the young people in terms of their well being and their feelings towards others – yet clearly these youth workers were both working *on* young people. With this in mind the importance of relationship does not preclude a youth worker from working *on* young people.
- In all situations learning was linked in some way to the value base of the youth worker/agency/institution of the youth worker. What was learnt was decided by the youth worker – but the youth workers were keen to involve the young person in the thought process. Essentially the learning had already been defined in some way by the youth worker's values and some sort of prior expert knowledge.
- The role of the youth workers and the behaviour of the young people did not reflect either equality or mutuality when it came to looking at the behaviour of the young people.
- In each scenario the youth worker is quite deliberate in their interventions whether responsive or predetermined. In some ways given the evidence provided in the scenarios the distinction between predetermined and responsive intervention is somewhat arbitrary given that neither are mutually exclusive.
- All of the youth workers cited here would have processed to varying degrees the situation they found themselves in with young people. In each scenario the youth worker is paying careful attention to the process, so as to achieve a desired outcome. In this respect the process is not at the expense of the outcome.

- In each situation the young person/people have choice but not all are encouraged to act autonomously. In the penultimate scenario the youth worker is allowed to take away the autonomy of the young person when she attempts to manage the feelings of the young person.
- The closest scenario to a dialectical approach is the first scenario where the youth worker tries to engage the young person in a process of reason and logic, however the young person chooses not to accept the idea that reason and consistency provide a valid path to truth.

## Perspective 2

- The needs of young people have already been intellectualised by a professional/political body.
- Predetermined knowledge of what people need results in the control of others.
- Youth work lacks transparency – practices such as reflection do not include young people.
- It is not possible for the youth worker to have a dialectical relationship with a young person, therefore the youth worker cannot work with a young person.
- Young people are always seen in deficit regardless of whether the youth worker is responding to the needs of young people or predetermining the needs of young people.
- All youth work follows an agenda that is outside of the control of the young person.

As with the first perspective, not all but some of the claims in the second perspective can be substantiated by practice.
- From the examples provided there is no evidence to suggest that the young person/people played any part in defining these values. With this in mind the youth worker can be thought of as someone who is trying to influence the values of young people.
- In each situation the youth worker was working from a position that it was the young person/people who needed to change in some way, whether it is in their attitudes or simply trying to see how as individuals the young people relate to each other. However there is also evidence that the youth worker could see the potential of the young person; moreover this became one of the aims of the youth worker, to develop the potential of the young person.
- None of the young people were fixed, but in all situations the young people were perceived in deficit at some point. Interestingly in the second scenario the young people did not always accept this label; moreover

they were willing to challenge the idea that they were in some way dependant on the youth worker.

– All the relationships were voluntary, no young people were coerced, none of the youth workers had any real control over the young people in the sense that they could make the young people act against their will. At any time the young person/people could have rejected the discourse that informed the interventions of the youth workers.

– Whilst it is clear that in all scenarios the youth worker has intellectualized to varying degrees the needs of the young person/people, there is no obvious correlation between the discourse that informs the youth workers and the control of the young person unless the young person is willing to accept being told what to think. In each of the scenarios the youth worker is not in a position to make the young person/people accept their discourse, this is up to the young person/people to decide.

– The issue of transparency and working on are not necessarily incompatible. It is possible to work *on* someone at the same time as being transparent about your aims and values.

– Whilst it is not possible for the youth worker to have a truly dialectical relationship with a young person because of their status and role there is no reason to avoid attempting to engage young people in a dialectical approach towards understanding as seen in the first and fourth scenarios.

To summarize, on the premise that the examples cited in this chapter broadly reflect the current context of youth work practice; it is not possible for youth workers to work *with* young people; but neither should working *on* young people be vilified as a youth work approach. The scenarios above have shown that in practice youth workers make ethical judgments that may be quite subtle in their response to the circumstances; at the same time the youth workers will not necessarily be able to justify their actions from the perspective of a more systematic ethical theory. The challenge for the final chapter is to identify at a theoretical level those ethical grounds which justify working *on* young people.

# SECTION 5

## PERSPECTIVES OF ETHICAL THEORY ON WORKING *ON* YOUNG PEOPLE

The purpose of this final chapter is to consider whether working *on* young people can be justified on a level of general principle. This is achieved by considering the scenarios presented thus far from the perspective of theoretical positions developed within moral philosophy. Essentially the first question is the same. Can one ethically justify working *on* young people? This will be considered from the perspectives of an ethic of care; utilitarian ethics; Kantian ethics; and Aristotelian ethics.

There a number of reasons why youth workers work *on* young people, some of which have been explored already. One reason that hasn't been mentioned explicitly is the idea that youth workers care for young people; moreover it is one's moral duty to care for others (Gilligan, 1982). Noddings argues that to care is natural; from natural care ethical care will emerge. (Flinders, 2001). Noddings does not reject the importance of reasoning; however she does argue that neither reasoning nor working out the right thing to do based on consequences will provide the right answer to ethical issues on their own. One is required to care.

From a feminist perspective Noddings elevates the natural instinct to care above reasoning and consequentialist thinking. Noddings (2005) suggests that there are four essential components to every caring situation: modeling – showing people how to care by actively caring; dialogue – open ended discussion where neither party knows at the outset where the discussion will go rather than as a pretence to persuading young people to accept what the youth worker is saying; practice - creating opportunities to care for; and confirmation – looking for the best in others.

Underpinning the ethic of care is the importance of developing and maintaining caring relationships. In the third scenario the youth worker demonstrates a level of concern for the well being of the young person when they talk about wanting the young person to feel safe and secure, they want the young person to be happy. Arguably such aims represent a caring approach to youth work. The youth worker cares about what happens to the young person. In addition the young person is happy to be helped. Whether wittingly or otherwise the young person approaches the youth worker because the youth worker can help. The youth worker is able *'to elicit a response that is congruent with an underlying need or desire'* Noddings (2005:17). Certainly the elements of working *on* which come out of the third scenario are recognised in the model that Noddings puts forward.

The relationship between the carer and the cared for is unequal. This is necessary on the premise that the cared for needs to be cared for, the cared for needs to be helped – however the purpose of helping is not to maintain the deficit relationship between cared and cared for, rather it is to improve the situation of the young person to a more satisfactory view of themselves (Buber, 1965:83ff ). This is where the practice of affirmation comes into play.

From a position of understanding that is cemented within a relationship the carer (youth worker), is able to identify the potential of the young person and work with the young person to help them recognise their potential. To be able to do this effectively the carer (youth worker), has to be able to attend to the needs of the young person, emptying themselves so as to be able to receive the young person (Noddings, 2005:16). In scenario 3 whilst the youth worker is constantly reflecting on what is best for the young person they are more likely to be effective if they have an accurate picture of what the young person is thinking/feeling. On the premise that the youth worker in scenario 3 is someone who instinctively cares for, who is able to attend to others, without prejudice or agenda, one can argue that they are working *on* the young person *for* the young person - without an agenda other than the moral imperative that one ought to care - where the main task of the youth worker is trying to see the world of the young person as the young person sees it. Whether this is feasible will depend on a number of factors. Firstly is it in the youth workers character to instinctively care. Secondly, does the young person want to or is the young person capable of receiving the care of the youth worker? Thirdly to what extent is the youth worker free to focus on the way the young person sees the world rather than seeking to impose a view of the world on the young person? And fourthly how accurately is the youth worker able to identify the potential of the young person?

From a normative position one is justified in working *on* young people *for* young people when based on a caring relationship between the youth worker and the young person, where the youth worker is following their natural instinct to help others, whilst focusing on both the need and the potential of the young person, thus respecting the young person as a means to an end in themselves.

The second ethical perspective to be considered, that provides a normative position for working *on* young people is utilitarianism – whereby actions are right insofar as they promote the welfare/wellbeing/flourishing of the greatest number and wrong when they do the opposite. With this in mind one is being asked to consider to what extent working *on* young people will contribute to the greatest amount of well being/flourishing/ welfare for the greatest number of people. The main issue here is the extent to which the individual liberty is affected in pursuit of the greater good. In response to this dilemma Mill (1975) states that allowing freedom to the individual, where the only restraint is against any act that restricts the freedom of another or harms another will result in social progress. Central to this process is a system that allows people to think and act freely, which in turn results in a concern for the happiness of others. This system is democracy, a process where people are happy because they are able to think freely, critique independently and contribute to the happiness of others through a process of ongoing debate. Mill (1975) also recognises that for such a system to be effective, people need to be educated.

Interestingly Mill questions the role of the state and education. Whilst the state should be responsible for ensuring that all people are educated to a sufficient level to be able to participate effectively in democracy rather than conforming to authority, there is also a concern that were the state to dictate what is taught, individuality and freedom become undermined (Mill 1975:98). Here one is being asked to consider an education that encourages independent critical thought.

If we look at the intervention of the youth worker in the second scenario in the previous chapter, in terms of utility, one could argue that by removing a particular group of young people from the streets and diverting their attention into positive activities, there will be greater happiness, the majority will cease to be disaffected by the behaviour of the minority. As an approach there is little evidence of democracy in that the thoughts and actions of the young people are not accepted by the youth worker. The intervention of the youth worker is not democratic in that the youth worker is constantly telling the young people how they should behave and the benefits that would be conferred by the state were they to conform. One way in which this might be justified is if it can be shown that the intervention of the youth worker formed part of an educational process that might ultimately result in the young people being able to think freely and critically for themselves.

From the information provided in this scenario there is no evidence to suggest that the young people were encouraged to think freely and critically about their circumstances. To achieve this level of choice the youth worker needed to engage the young people, getting them to think about their circumstances and what it was that they wanted for themselves and how what they wanted might make a contribution to the happiness of others. They were given a choice and the youth worker made every attempt to be transparent in his intervention, however the choice was a negative one, essentially do this or else.

From a Millian perspective of utilitarianism one can justify working *on* young people providing working *on* is geared towards the freedom and liberty of young people to think critically, who in turn will respect the rights of others to do the same. In general working *on* young people *for* young people should have good consequences that encourage people to develop autonomy, which means letting them make their own choices and participate in choices made about them.

The third normative position to be considered is Kant's central claim that one should never treat other people merely as a means to an end. The important word in this phrase is merely. Arguably it is impossible not to treat people as a means to an end, most relationships are based on the premise that you will benefit in some way from the other person involved in the relationship.

> *What the Humanity formula rules out is engaging in this pervasive use of Humanity in such a way that we treat it as a mere means to our ends.*
> Johnson 2008: http://plato.stanford.edu/entries/kant-moral/

Essentially what Kant is saying is that one should also recognise and treat people as means to their own ends; that is, respecting the humanity of the individual and the capacity of the individual to act autonomously, to be able to reason and behave rationally:

> *Second, it is not human beings per se but the 'Humanity' in human beings that we must treat as an end in itself. Our 'Humanity' is that collection of features that make us distinctively human, and these include capacities to engage in self-directed rational behavior and to adopt and pursue our own ends, and any other capacities necessarily connected with these.*
> Johnson 2008: http://plato.stanford.edu/entries/kant-moral/

Here one needs to consider the extent to which the young person is encouraged to exercise their rational capacities and to what extent the youth worker is working towards a better life for the young people concerned. There is a balance to be struck here. In both the first and second scenarios we can see that the youth worker had a basic idea of what the desired outcome was to be. In the first scenario it was that the young person recognized the need to change their racist attitudes and in the second scenario it was that the young people stopped causing trouble on their local estate. Here we have two situations where the behaviour of the young person/people was not to be respected. With this in mind it would be easy to argue that some sort of intervention was required that in some way prevented the young person/ people from continuing in their abusive/disruptive behaviour.

The question here is whether such an intervention respects their autonomy, to treat them in the way that you think is good for them, when you think that you know better than them? Violating the autonomy of a young person

and interfering in their freedom in order to advance their welfare is pater-
nalistic (Dworkin, 1988:128). Whilst the first two scenarios suggest that
the youth worker had already decided what the outcome ought to be, it
was in the first scenario that one gets a greater sense that the youth worker
respected the autonomy of the young person, given their willingness to
provide an opportunity for the young person to question and rationalize
their own behaviour.

In terms of justifying working *on* the young person *for* the young person
from a Kantian perspective one would need to be able to show that at some
point in the relationship between the young person and the youth worker,
the young person is encouraged to rationalize, to reason, to recognise their
own a priori capacity to reason out their experiences (Stumpf, 1971:293).
However the importance of being given the opportunity to rationalize and
reason is not simply a matter of freedom from interference.

The final ethical theory to be considered is the Aristotelian perspective
of virtue. The person who is able to exercise practical reason so as to see
the way in which they ought to behave is from an Aristotelian perspective
*being* virtuous. Aristotle suggests that we have an irrational part of the soul
which is susceptible to external forces like love and hate, things that lead
one to desire or things that lead one to run away or reject – without rational
thinking these behaviors could manifest wildly (Stumpf 1971). Virtue exists
when the individual is able to rationally control the natural response we
have to external forces. Virtue is the mean between our extremes. Aristotle
goes on to argue that to be virtuous one must be able to deliberate about
one's action so as to know what the right thing to do is. Understanding and
choosing the right thing to do and then acting upon one's decision is what
makes us virtuous. To be virtuous requires practice. Being virtuous will be
different in different situations. To be acting virtuously it is essential that
we carry out our act:
- knowingly
- by choice
- for its own sake
- from a 'virtuous disposition', i.e. as part of what one might call our
  *character*.

As seen already there is evidence to suggest that the workers in the first
two scenarios were attempting to get the young person/people to rationalize
their behaviour. In the first scenario the youth worker was quite deliberate
in their attempts to get the young person to understand the inconsistency in
their thinking; moreover the youth worker was of the view that through
rationalizing and understanding the young person would come to the right
conclusion. Whilst less obvious there were signs of this taking place in the

second scenario where the youth worker wanted the young people to rationalize their own desires in relation to the expectation of others. In the third scenario there was no evidence that the youth worker wanted the young person to rationalize their behaviour. Instead the youth worker modeled care, she showed interest in the young person and without wishing to cause too much distress for the young person, the youth worker attempted to show empathy. In many respects the youth worker reinforced Noddings' earlier assertion that reasoning and consequentialist thinking alone will not provide the right answers. Finally in the last scenario the youth worker was challenging the way in which the young people felt about each other and at the same time trying to get the young people to rationalize their feelings towards each other. From an Aristotelian point of view, working *on* young people *for* young people is justified in so far as the intervention is aimed at the development of the ability to rationalize their actions as part of a process that is aimed at being virtuous; moreover this is something that can and should be learnt and practiced (Stumpf, 1971:100)

# SECTION 6

## CONCLUSION

In many respects the answer to the overall question can youth workers work *with* young people is no. However this needn't be a cause for concern. As seen in the previous chapter there are a number of ethical theories that justify working *on* young people for the benefit of young people. Youth workers will always be in situations where they have to work *on*; which might include restricting choice, maintaining boundaries in relation to behaviour and societal norms. However working *on* can also be based on a potentiality model, the youth worker needn't be coercive, and intervention can be both responsive and of a fostering nature. Perhaps a more accurate description is that at times the youth worker may not always be in role. In such moments the youth worker might find themselves '*being*' (Fromm 1979:42), with young people, but not as someone who is working, rather they are able to share in the experience of the young person. Depending on the role of the youth worker there will be some fluctuation between the amounts of time the youth worker finds themselves being with the young person and the amount of time they are working *on* the young person.

On a separate note one might also wish to consider the precedent created in this thesis which encourages one to question the normative values that inform the field of youth work. Essentially the approach taken with this thesis provides an example of the kind of construct that is inherent and needs to be unearthed within the body and knowledge of youth work. In Foucaultian terms what has transpired is an archeological analysis of youth work discourse which considers those discursions that have been kept and discarded so as to inform current youth work discourse (Gutling, 2003).

In attempting to set a precedent for critical philosophical enquiry within the field of youth work one would hope that those who claim to work *with* rather than *on* young people will begin to consider their reasons for making this distinction. Arguably to claim to only work *with* young people is somewhat arbitrary. In wanting to do the best for young people, there is a sense that youth workers want to be able to frame their practice in a way that avoids negative connotations, for example not wanting to be seen as coercive or manipulative, instead being seen to respect young people and foster choice.

In coming to an end it is clear that this thesis is in no way a finite piece of work. In looking to build on the themes generated within this thesis there is still a need to explore the legitimacy of the youth worker as someone who identifies those young people whose needs aren't being addressed by families, education, community, peers and so on. Whilst there are clear calls to respond to the needs of young people from the state, religious groups, community groups and the voluntary sector; it is also worth considering whether those needs could be better served by other relationships within the young people's local community, family, peers and so on. To explore this phenomenon more fully one would have to consider whether there is a need for youth work; with this in mind one line of questioning closes and another opens.

Aquinas, T. (1920 [1273]). *The Summa Theologica of St. Thomas Aquinas* (2nd and Rev. ed., Fathers of the English Dominican Province, Trans.).

Barnett, S. A. (1884). *Settlements of university men in great towns*. A paper read at St John's, Oxford on 17th November 1883. Oxford: The Chronicle Company. Reprinted in Pimlott, J. A. R. (1935). *Toynbee Hall. Fifty years of social progress 1884–1934* (pp. 266–273). London: J. M. Dent.

Barrett-Lennard, G. T. (1998). *Carl Roger's helping syste. Journey and substance*. London: Sage Publications.

Barrow, R., & Woods, R. (1988). *An introduction to philosophy of education*. London: Routledge Falmer.

Blundell, M. (2008). Retrieved from http://www.salmoncentre.co.uk/

Callan, E. (1994). Autonomy and alienation. *Journal of Philosophy of Education, 28*(1).

Callan, E., & White, J. (2005). In N. Blake, et al. (Eds.), *The Blackwell guide to the philosophy of education*. Malden, MA: Blackwell Publishing.

Collinson, D., & Plant, K. (1987). *Fifty major philosophers*. London: Routledge.

Cuypers, S. (1995). What Wittgenstein would have said about personal autonomy. *Studies in Philosophy and Education, 14*(2–3).

Davies, B. (1999). *From voluntaryism to welfare state a history of the youth service in England Volume 1 1939–1979*. London: National Youth Agency.

Davies, B. (2005a). Youth Work: A Manifesto for our Times. *Youth and Policy*, No. 88, pp. 5–28.

Davies, B. (2005b). If youth matters, where is the youth work?. *Youth and Policy*, No. 89, pp. 21–26.

Dworkin, G. (1988). *The theory and practice of autonomy*. Cambridge: Cambridge University Press.

DfES. (2006). *Positive activities for young people*. Cardiff: CRG Research Limited.

Egan, G. (1994). *The skilled helper*. California: Brooks/Cole Publishing Company.

Feinstein, L., et al. (2005). *Leisure contexts in adolescence and their effects on adult outcomes*. London: Centre for Research on the Wider Benefits of Learning, Institute of Education.

Flinders, D. J. (2001). Nel Noddings. In J. A. Palmer (Ed.), *Fifty modern thinkers on education. From Piaget to the present*. London: Routledge.

Foucault, M. (2003). *Society must be defended: Lectures at the College de France*. New York: St Martins Press.

Fromm, E. (2005). *To have or to be (originally published in 1979)*. London: Continuum.

Gadotti, M. (1996). *Pedagogy of Praxis A dialectical; Philosophy of education*. New York: State University of New York Press.

Gilligan, C. (1982). *In a different voice*. Cambridge, MA: Harvard University Press.

Goetchius, G., & Tash, M. J. (1967). *Working with unattached youth: Problem, approach, method*. London: Routledge and Kegan Paul.

Gordon, P., & White, J. (1979). *Philosphers as educational reformers*. London: Routledge and Kegan Paul.

Gutling, G. (2003). *Michel Foucault*. Retrieved from http://plato.stanford.edu/entries/foucault

Habermas, J. (1984). *Theory of communicative action: Vol. 1 Reason and the rationalisation of society.* Boston: Beacon Hall.

Hayter, S. (2003). *Can youth work be fully accountable, Young People Now.* London: Haymarket Publishing.

Hirsch, J. (2002). *A place to call home.* Washington, DC: American Psychological Association.

Illich, I. (1971). *Deschooling society.* New York: Harper and Row.

Jeffs, T. (2001). *"Something to give and much to learn": Settlements and youth work.* In R. Gilchrist & T. Jeffs (Eds.), *Settlements, social change and community action.* London: Jessica Kingsley.

Johnson, R. (2008). Retrieved from http://plato.stanford.edu/entries/kant-moral/

May, L. (1992). *Sharing responsibility, cited.* In T. Honderich (Ed.), (1995). *The Oxford companion to philosophy.* Oxford: Oxford University Press.

McNair, S. (1996). Learning autonomy in a changing world. In R. Edwards, et al. (Eds.), *Boundaries of adult learning.* London: Routledge and Open University Press.

Mill, J. S. (1975). *On liberty.* New York: Norton and Company Inc.

Noddings, N. (2005). *The challenge to care in schools: An alternative approach to education.* New York: Teachers College Press.

Pring, R. A. (1995). *Closing the gap, liberal education and vocational preparation.* London: Hodder & Stoughton.

Pusey, M. (1987). *Jurgen Habermas.* London: Tavistock Publications.

Peters, R. S. (1981). *Essays on educators.* London: George Allen & Unwin Limited.

Peters, R. S. (1971). *Ethics and education.* London: George Allen & Unwin Limted.

Pink, T. (2003). *Free Will.* Oxford: Oxford University Press.

Rogers, C. (1967). *On becoming a person. A therapist's view of psychotherapy.* London: Constable.

Schön, D. (1983). *The reflective practitioner. How professionals think in action.* London: Temple Smith.

Smart, B. (1985). *Michel Foucault.* London: Tavistock Publications.

Smith, M. K., & Smith, H. (2007). *The art of helping others.* London: Jessica Kingsley.

Smith, M. K., & Smith, H. (2006). *Working with individuals.* Canning Town: YMCA George Williams College.

Smith, M. K. (1999, 2002). Youth work: An introduction. *The Encyclopedia of Informal Education.* Retrieved from www.infed.org/youthwork/b-yw/htm. Last updated 2007.

Spence, J. (2006). *Youth work: Voices of practice.* Leicester: National Youth Agency.

Standish, P. (2002). Education without aims cited. In R. Marples (Eds.), *The aims of education.* New York: Routledge.

Strauss, L., & Crapsey, J. (1963). *History of political philosophy.* Chicago: Round McNally Publishing.

Stumpf, S. E. (1971). *Philosophy history and problems.* New York: McGraw-Hill Book Company.

Taylor, P. (1993). *The texts of Paulo Freire.* Buckingham: Open University Press.

Tiffany, G. (2003). *Relationships and learning.* In M. Wolfe & L. Richardson (Eds.), *Principles and practices of informal education.* London: Routledge Falmer.

White, J. (1990). *Education and the good life: Beyond the national curriculum.* London: Kogan Page.

White, P. (1996). *Civic virtues and public schooling, educating citizens for a democratic society.* New York: Teachers College Press.

Young, K. (1999). *The art of youth work.* Dorset: Russell House Publishing.

Youth Work Ireland. (2008). Retrieved from http://www.youthworkgalway.ie/

Lightning Source UK Ltd.
Milton Keynes UK
05 May 2010

153789UK00001B/31/P